IMAGES
of America

THE NORTH SHORE
OF LAKE TRAVIS

The one-room schoolhouse, Cox Springs School, is being restored in honor of the early pioneers' spirit and dedication to frontier education. Under the direction of the North Shore Heritage and Cultural Society, the schoolhouse has been painted and reroofed. The North Shore Heritage and Cultural Society historic marker was placed on the schoolhouse in April 2009. (Courtesy of Shirley Davis.)

ON THE COVER: Rose Marie (left), the daughter of Gilbert and "Bunce" Ballerstedt, and her friend Cecil Rennerly, visited from Austin in 1941. The girls were enchanted by the endless beauty of Lake Travis as it rose at Arkansas Bend. (Courtesy of the Ballerstedt family.)

IMAGES
of America

THE NORTH SHORE
OF LAKE TRAVIS

The North Shore Heritage and
Cultural Society

ARCADIA
PUBLISHING

Published by Arcadia Publishing
Charleston, South Carolina

Library of Congress Control Number: 2009930175

For all general information contact Arcadia Publishing at:
Telephone 843-853-2070
Fax 843-853-0044
E-mail sales@arcadiapublishing.com
For customer service and orders:
Toll-Free 1-888-313-2665

Visit us on the Internet at www.arcadiapublishing.com

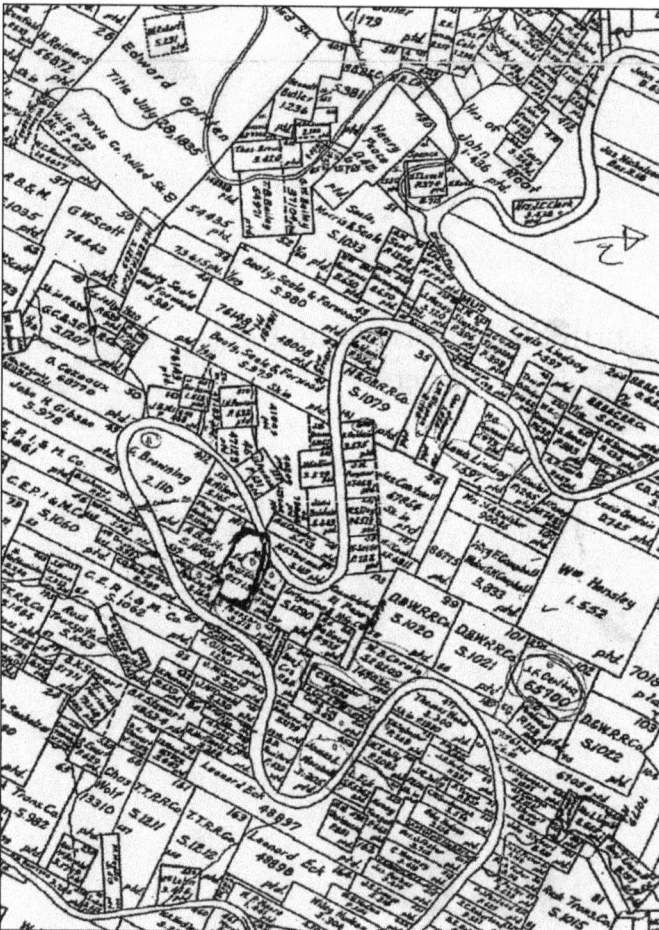

This book is dedicated to the early settlers of the North Shore of Lake Travis. The land grant homesteaders map depicts the owners and the location of homesteads. (Courtesy of Texas State Land Board.)

CONTENTS

ACKNOWLEDGMENTS

This book celebrates the people who settled, founded, and nourished the North Shore of Lake Travis from its inception to today. The North Shore Heritage and Cultural Society's gratitude goes to the people who helped with the research, compilation of data and sharing of their photographs.

A special thank you goes to the North Shore Heritage and Cultural Society team. An additional thank you goes to Arcadia Publishing, the Preston Carlton family, Dan and Shirley Davis, Joe and Claretta England, Amparro Giller, the Jones family, the Johnson family, Genny Kercheville, Karen Kilfeather, Carla Lott, Janice Hollingsworth McGrew, the Red and Rose Olander family, Mike Parker (the *North Lake Travis LOG*), Gloria Van Cleave, John and Charlene Vohs, and Vasara Photography.

One of the most rewarding aspects of working on this book was the opportunity to share with people the stories and pictures that together document the history of the North Shore of Lake Travis.

Janice (Hollingsworth) McGrew (top left) and Genny (Rodgers) Kercheville (top right) represent descendants of early North Shore land grant and ranch families. Newcomers John and Charlene Vohs (pictured at bottom) join in the celebration of a shared future and ongoing spirit for positive change. (Courtesy of Vasara Photography.)

INTRODUCTION

In February 1810, the migrating golden-cheeked warblers heading for their nesting grounds in central Texas would have seen a vista unlike the one the North Shore of Lake Travis now presents. Trees were few, mostly along waterways, and prairie grass was abundant. The mature Ashe juniper (locally known as cedar) provided the strips of bark required for nesting materials by the warbler. No railroads, highways, or major structures existed. The Colorado River twisted through the landscape, resembling an artist's uncertain stroke. Tonkawa, Lipan Apache, Comanche, and Kiowa tribes hunted, fought, and enjoyed the subtropical weather. No doubt they wondered at the occasional dinosaur track. They saw and examined fossils deposited when a shallow sea covered the area. The Native Americans themselves contributed to the heritage of the area through relics, tools, burial sites, and other items still being discovered today.

Legislative establishment of Travis County in 1840 activated a new era for the North Shore. Prior to that event, Stephen F. Austin had received impresario contracts from Mexico to settle families in Texas. In 1831, he had received one for the settlement of 800 families. This was known as the upper colony, and included the areas now known as Jonestown, Lago Vista, and Point Venture. Some of the early heroes braving the sometimes inimical conditions of the North Shore were Noah Smithwick, John Henry Lohmann, Samuel and Ed Pearson, Caleb and Thomas Sylvester, and James Carlton. Mills were established on the Colorado River, first by Mormon settlers, then by Noah Smithwick. Industry had come to the area.

The years during and after the Civil War brought dissension and economic hardship to the North Shore. Unionists and Secessionists argued, and slaves passed through, seeking paths to freedom. Settlers built homes, farm buildings, and fences on land destined to become the Balcones Canyonlands National Wildlife Refuge (BCNWR)—a future home for the descendants of the golden-cheeked warbler.

By the late 1890s, those living in the North Shore area had learned to respect the Colorado River. Much-needed support existed on the south side of the river: supplies, cotton gins, doctors, and more. When the river was benign, fords were usable, and several existed. If the river was not cooperating, alternative routes were long and difficult.

Progress was on the way. Acquisitions of large tracts of land occurred. Richard Rodgers purchased more than 22,000 acres of land and named the tract "Sunset Ranch." A meteorite had been found in that area in 1889 and scientifically reported in 1890. Scientific interest in finding the site of that meteorite led to more finds on the ranch in later years.

The Hensels purchased land and built the first two-story, stone-block house in the area. Schools and churches were important, and the first school, a one-room cabin, was called Cox Springs School and was first located on land near Lohmann's Ford.

Recurring floods on the Colorado River resulted in the establishment of the Lower Colorado River Authority in the 1930s, and eventually, construction of a series of dams was begun. The completion of Mansfield Dam in the early 1940s resulted in the formation of Lake Travis.

The presence and beauty of this flood-control lake forever changed the direction and speed of development of the North Shore. A bridge built at Lohmann's Ford was forgotten as Lake Travis filled. Previously, residents in the area had been able to take goods to market in the Bee Caves area just across the bridge. Without the use of the bridge, more difficult and lengthy roads had to be found.

Irish "cedar choppers" moved in to harvest the then-abundant junipers. Construction workers for various projects discovered the North Shore and remained after the work was finished. World War II veterans returned and settled. Developers took a strong interest in the beauty of the Hill Country and the recreational value of Lake Travis. Lago Vista proper began to emerge from the development activities of John Moss, Dr. C. Paul Harris, Sid Wheless, Newt Johnson, National Homes, Inc., and a resort developer from Japan. Warren and Emmitt Jones similarly developed what is now Jonestown.

Highways from Austin to the North Shore were primitive and unpaved at first. Personal contacts and requests to legislators and officials eventually resulted in the roads being paved. Later the major road to the area was widened and straightened. With improved access, interest in the area increased. Eventually, bus transportation was available.

In the mid-1980s, Lago Vista and Jonestown each incorporated as cities. Weather continued to surprise residents, with a major flood on December 25, 1991. High-dollar homes became common. Proposed new developments were scrutinized by the architectural committees of the cities. A post office was built in Lago Vista. Many retail businesses provide necessary goods and services.

The golden-cheeked warbler can now nest in the BCNWR with little fear of danger. An annual bird festival is popular with area residents and visitors. Other events now take place on the North Shore for the pleasure and entertainment of all, such as the International Bicycle Race, the Memorial Day sailboat race, Hill Country Days, the Fourth of July celebration, various golf tournaments, and Jonestown events. In the Travis Peak area, the Flat Creek Winery and the Hensel Camp draw visitors.

Not to be forgotten are the notable people who live in the area, including Marge Richards, who at 95 is the only living daughter of a Civil War veteran in Texas. Many of the descendants of the early settlers have kept the North Shore as their home. Many have contributed to this product, and their contributions are cherished.

One

WILD LANDS

Friendly and welcoming were not terms that would be applied to the Central Texas landscape in the 1800s. Fossils from marine animals that once lived in the shallow sea that covered that area were neighbors to implements left by prehistoric peoples and to bones of extinct animals. (Courtesy of University of Texas Press.)

Not officially authenticated as dinosaur tracks, the origin of these formations has long been a mystery to viewers. This photograph of formations found in the streambed of Cow Creek shows just one of many such puzzles in the North Lake Travis area. (Courtesy of North Shore Heritage and Cultural Society.)

Objects such as flint arrowheads, scrapers, and stone grinders are evidence of early migrating people who lived in this area from 9,000 BCE to around 2,000 BCE. In 1982, the Paleo-Indian woman Leanne was found in the Leander area. In 2006, a skeleton between 700 and 2,000 years old was found on the banks of Lake Travis near Pace Bend. (Courtesy of Genevieve Kercheville.)

This carving made on a buffalo scapula depicts an encounter between two armed Spaniards and a mounted Comanche warrior. In 1716, the Spanish Ramon–St. Denis party explored this area to establish a mission. (Courtesy of Bureau of American Ethnology, Smithsonian Institution.)

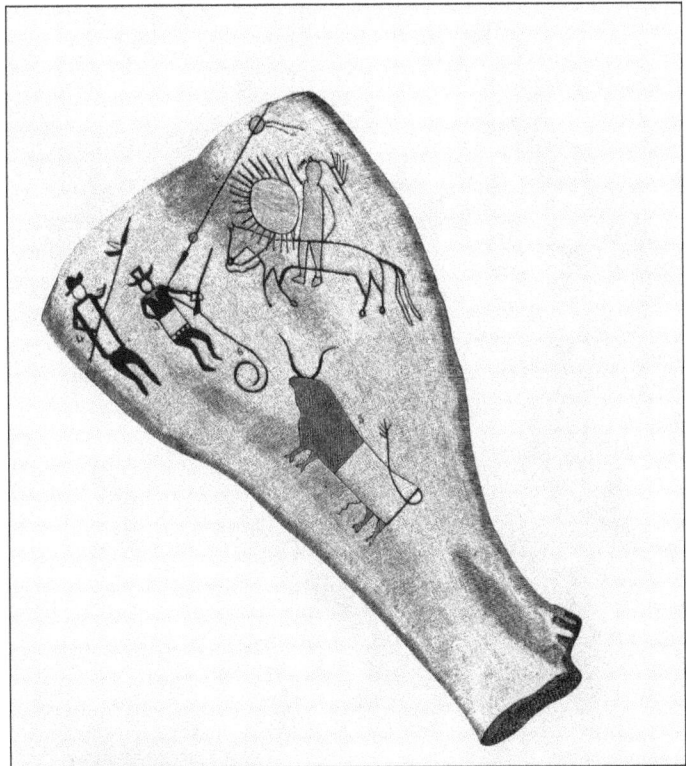

Early settlers to the area found themselves trying to coexist with at least four Native American groups: Kiowa, Comanche, Tonkawa, and Lipan Apache. The Kiowas, with a long history of agricultural achievements, had made peace in 1806 with their former enemies, the Comanches, who were hunters. A Kiowa father and his daughters are shown here. The Tonkawas, also hunters, were thought to use the unique method of driving their prey off high precipices to their death. The Lipan Apaches, adept at tracking among other skills, resisted the intrusion into their lands by fighting the settlers and attacking Spanish missions. (Courtesy of Eugene C. Barker Texas History Collection, Center for American History, University of Texas at Austin.)

11

Quanah Parker, the last chief of the Comanches, led his people in the Texas Red River War, which ended in 1875. Foreseeing impossible situations for the Comanches if fighting continued, Chief Parker surrendered and led his followers on a new path to the "white man's road." The son of a Comanche chief and Cynthia Ann Parker, a white woman captured by the Comanches in 1836, Quanah Parker eventually became a successful rancher and a shrewd businessman. (Courtesy of National Anthropological Archives, Smithsonian Institution, neg. 56, 374.)

Although other Native American tribes were established in Central Texas before the Kiowas arrived, the Kiowas enjoyed outstanding leadership. Chief Satanta (pronounced Set-t'ain-te and meaning White Bear) was a warrior, negotiator, and orator, among other skills. He was known as "the Orator of the Plains" by American observers. Chief Satanta signed a treaty with the federal government in 1867 obliging the Kiowas to settle on a reservation. Under the provisions of the treaty, however, hunters were occasionally permitted to leave the reservation. These hunts sometimes became raids on Texas settlers and wagon trains. Eventually, Chief Satanta was arrested and imprisoned. (Courtesy of Eugene C. Barker Texas History Collection, Center for American History, University of Texas at Austin.)

The Comanches were known as great warriors. Pioneers who settled the Hopewell Community will always be remembered as the opponents of the last Comanche raid. Some of the settlers, Wofford and Mary Johnson and their daughter, were buried in the Hopewell Cemetery. (Courtesy of North Shore Heritage and Cultural Society.)

Many early Native American tribes lived along the Colorado River, and many types of arrowheads spanning different time periods have been found. The Bell type of arrowhead is from the Middle Archaic period, between 7,000 and 5,000 BCE. The Bonham or Sabinal type is from the Woodland to Mississippi periods, between 1,200 and 600 BCE. Marshall arrowheads date from the Middle Archaic to Woodland periods, between 6,000 and 2,000 BCE. The Nolan type is from the Middle Archaic period, between 6,000 and 4,000 BCE. Pedernales arrowheads come from the Middle Archaic to Woodland periods, between 6,000 and 2,000 BCE. Exotic forms of arrowheads are from the Middle Archaic to Mississippian periods, between 5,000 and 1,000 BCE. (Courtesy of Craig McGrew.)

Stephen Fuller Austin (1793–1836) is known today as "The Father of Texas" because of his success in recruiting people to settle in the area now known as Texas. His father, Moses Austin, had obtained a grant of land and permission to settle 300 families in the Mexican Texas area. Unfortunately, Moses Austin died before he could effect the colonization plan, and Stephen F. Austin assumed responsibility for the enterprise. The Upper Colony (1831), the last of five colonies established by him, included the settlements along the Colorado River. (Courtesy of Texas State Library and Archives Commission).

Two

HUMBLE HEROES

Evolution of a State by Noah Smithwick, one of North Shore's humble heroes, is regarded as the best of all books about life in early Texas. Smithwick's early successes distinguished him as a fluent translator for multiple Native American tribes from Tennessee to Texas before he turned 20. His lifetime of successes includes his designation as a Texas war hero and his work as a Texas Ranger and advocate for Native Americans. (Courtesy of Texas State Library and Archives Commission.)

General Location of Sites on the North Shore of Lake Travis

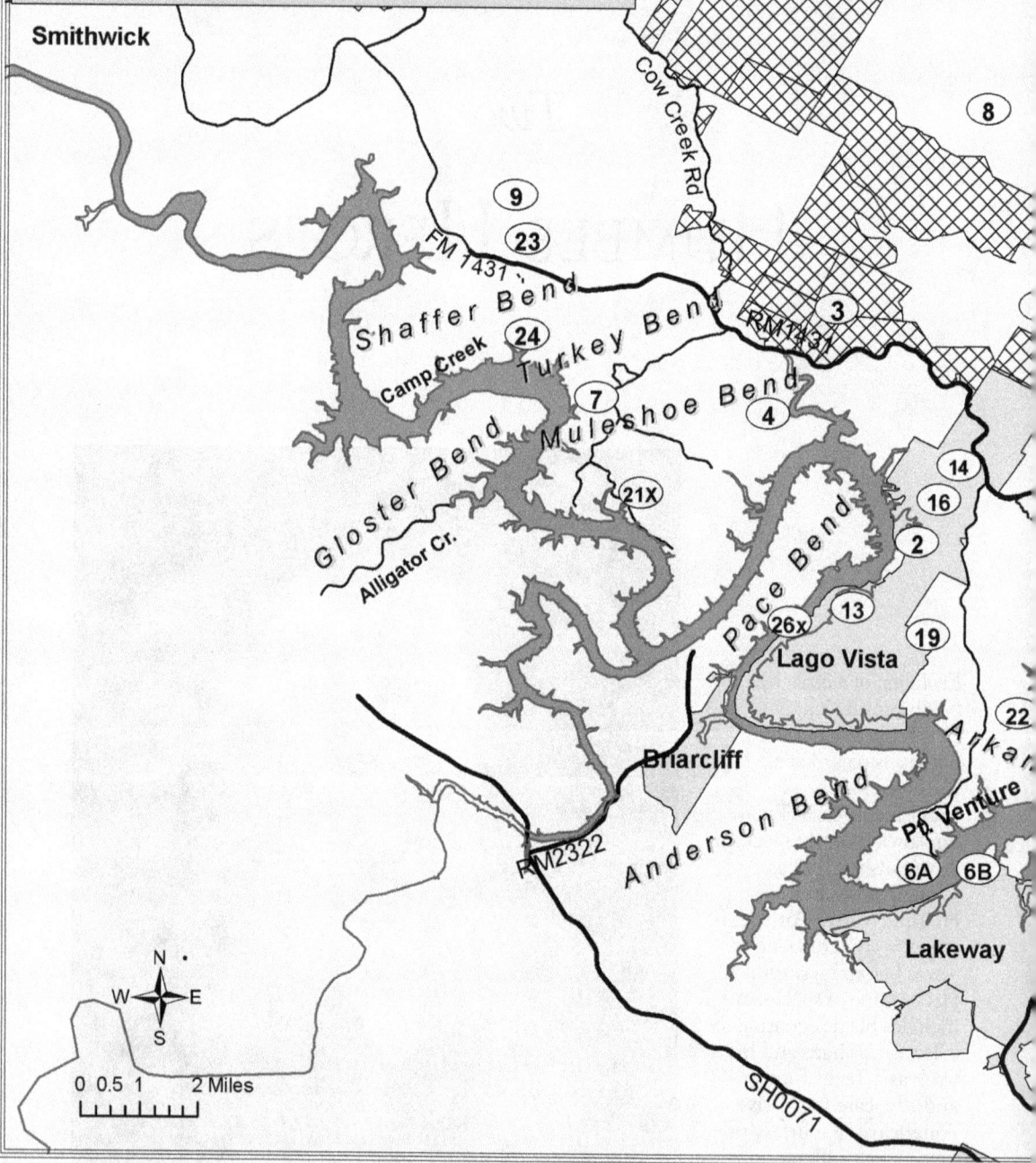

Smithwick

CR 284

8

Cow Creek Rd

9

23

FM 1431

Shaffer Bend

Camp Creek

24

Turkey Bend

RM 1431

3

7

Muleshoe Bend

4

Gloster Bend

14

16

Alligator Cr.

21X

Pace Bend

2

26x

13

19

Lago Vista

22

Arka...

Briarcliff

Anderson Bend

Pt. Venture

6A

6B

RM2322

Lakeway

N
W   E
S

0 0.5 1   2 Miles

SH0071

CR 281

nd Mountain

CR 279

Highway 183

Bagdad

Leander

18

Cedar Park

Trail's End Rd

11

12

5   10

Jonestown

25x

Brushy Creek

RM2769

rnett Rd

RM0620

Austin

Hudson Bend

RM2222

17

Round Mountain

Sites

Balcones Canyonlands NWR

Local roads

Tx_Citylimits

Cave

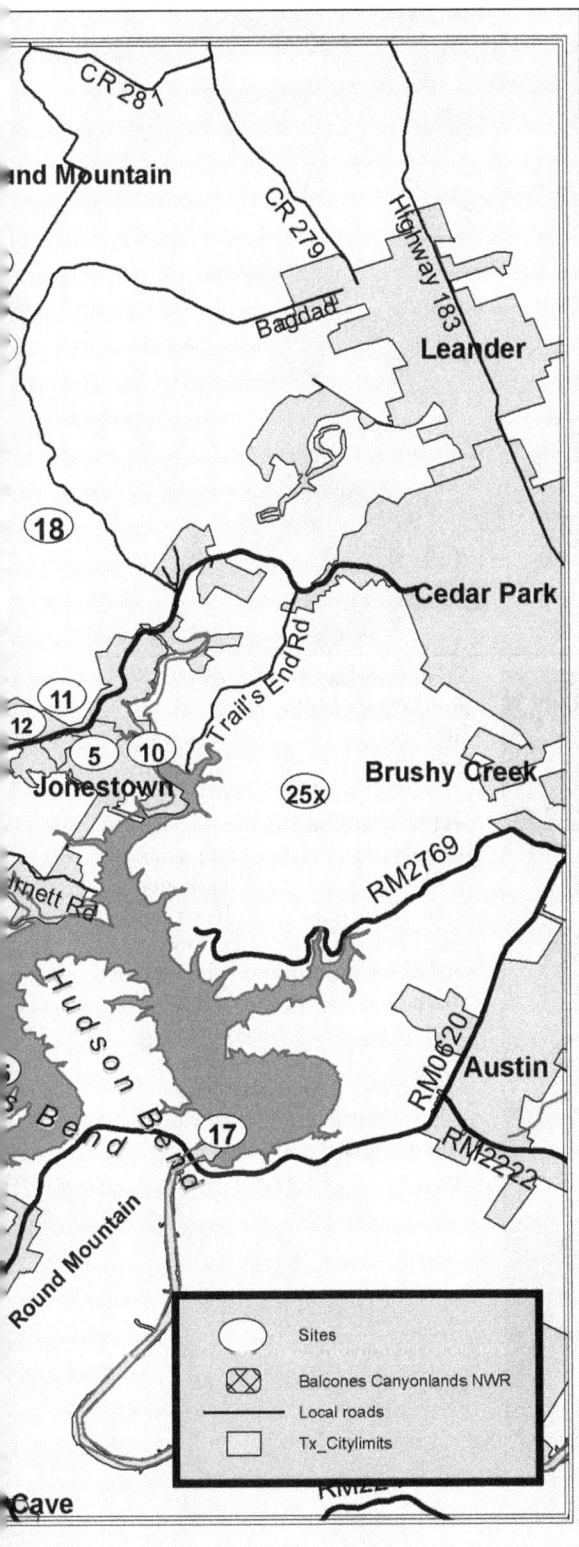

This map indicates the historical and modern sites along the Colorado River in the area that is currently called the North Shore of Lake Travis. Identified on the map are the following locations: 1. Air Power Museum; 2. Bar-K; 3. BCNWR; 4. Cow Creek and Hubbard's Cove; 5. Cox Springs School; 6a. Dink Pearson Park; 6b. Lohmann's Crossing; 7. Hensel's Christian Camp, Travis Peak Rock School, Church of Christ, Hensel's home, and Pioneer Memorial Cemetery; 8. Hopewell Cemetery; 9. Henry Thomas Lodge; 10. Jones Brothers Park; 11. Jonestown Veterans Memorial Park; 12. Jonestown Water Cistern; 13. Lago Vista Golf Course; 14. L. V. Swim Complex; 15. Lakeshore Ranch; 16. Little Red Schoolhouse; 17. Mansfield Dam; 18. Nameless School, Cemetery, and Ranch Gates; 19. Pearson's Ranch; 20. Round Mountain School House; 21. Singleton Cemetery; 22. Simpson Cemetery; 23. Smithwick Cemetery; 24. Smithwick Mill; 25. site where prehistoric Leander Lady was found; 26. site where prehistoric man was found; and 27. Sunset Ranch's original entrance. (Courtesy of North Shore Heritage and Cultural Society.)

Noah Smithwick believed that Smithwick's Mill would mark his fame. As the Civil War was waged throughout the Hill Country, his opposition to the Confederacy grew, and he was compelled to depart his beloved Texas for California. As documented in his book, many slaves departed Austin by crossing the Colorado River, and they settled communities on the North Shore. The emancipated slaves became prized in areas as skilled tradesmen, bulldoggers, doctors, and lawyers. (Above, courtesy of Bob Grain; left, courtesy of University of Texas Press.)

The Henry Thomas Lodge pays tribute to Noah Smithwick. (Above, courtesy of Donald A. Eatter; below, courtesy of Janet Lewis Crain.)

HENRY THOMAS LODGE, A.F. & A.M.
IN SETTLEMENT STARTED BY NOAH SMITHWICK, WHEN HE BUILT WATER MILL HERE IN 1855. IN 1861 HE MOVED TO CALIFORNIA, BUT THE MILL CONTINUED IN OPERATION.
A. M. COX ERECTED THIS BUILDING IN 1874. MINISTER HENRY THOMAS MOVED THE LODGE (CHARTERED JUNE 15, 1865) FROM TURKEY BEND, TEXAS, TO THIS PLACE IN 1876. A STORE OCCUPIED THE LOWER FLOOR.
LODGE OBTAINED UPPER STORY AT DEATH OF MR. COX, BY HIS WILL. F.P. LEWIS GAVE LOWER STORY IN 1952.
RECORDED TEXAS HISTORIC LANDMARK—1967

James N. Carlton of Virginia married Nancy Missouri Wiggins in Alabama in 1857. They had two small sons, John Burleson and James Franklin Carlton. James N. Carlton was killed during the Civil War at the Battle of Cedar Creek in Virginia in 1864. (Courtesy of Marjorie Carlton Simons.)

Nancy Missouri Wiggins (1839–1909), the widow of J. N. Carlton, came to Texas in 1865 with her two sons and her parents. She married Wilson Pope in 1867 and came to Travis County in 1873, where they settled in Cherry Hollow. She was the mother of nine more children. Nancy Wiggins Carlton Pope died at age 70 and was buried at the Nameless Cemetery. The Carlton family continues to live on the North Shore. (Courtesy of Marjorie Carlton Simons.)

Albert and Melvina Merck Lohmann stand with their youngest son, Bob, in 1900. Albert (1862–1940), who was the youngest of John Henry Lohmann's 21 children, was said to be 6 feet, 5 inches tall and could speak three languages— German, Spanish, and English. He played the fiddle well, and most of his nine children played an instrument. Most Sunday evenings, friends and family came to his house to play music. (Courtesy of Margaret Lohmann Holloway.)

The Albert Lohmann family bought property located on Long Hollow Creek, a tributary of Sandy Creek. He and his family lived in the barn for two years until he could get his house built. He farmed the land and raised livestock. He also served as justice of the peace and as trustee for the Round Mountain School Board. (Courtesy of Margaret Lohmann Holloway.)

The rich soil along the Colorado River was highly valued. The Lohmanns, Carltons, Pearsons, and Simpsons were fortunate to have land grants near its banks. (Courtesy of the Ballerstedt family.)

Fossils from the Glen Rose Limestone formation were created when the waters of the Gulf of Mexico covered this area. The fossils are estimated to be 110 million years old. The heart-shaped fossils are clam steinkerns and are called "deer hearts" by locals. The others are snail steinkerns. Many times these jewels were used to mark mound graves. (Courtesy of Genevieve Kercheville.)

Many family gatherings would have occurred under this ancient oak tree near the home of the Simpson family. Much of the Simpson pioneer homestead sits nobly among the numerous Spanish oaks surrounding and protecting the Simpson Cemetery, their home, and ranch lands. (Courtesy of North Shore Heritage and Cultural Society.)

The Simpson homestead, located near Sylvester Ford Drive, remains an excellent example of early land grant settlers' way of life. Hand-hewed logs bear the prints of the original builder. Natural resources were used to build the home. Cedar and oak trees, limestone and granite rocks, sea shells and fossil remains from prehistoric times, and native plants and seeds brought to Texas were utilized by the rugged settlers. Water from the nearby Colorado River was essential. (Courtesy of North Shore Heritage and Cultural Society.)

James Franklin Carlton (1862–1928) and Francis Ann Levitt (1860–1923) married and settled in the Valley of Sandy Creek. He built his home with a long porch and a dog run in the middle. An artesian water well was just outside the yard. Their grandchildren are, from left to right, Preston, Margie, and Peggy, who loved to visit there. (Courtesy of Marjorie Carlton Simons.)

Cousins J. J. (left) and Leslie Carlton proudly show off their buck deer in front of the well and corral at the J. F. Carlton homestead. (Courtesy of Marjorie Carlton Simons.)

24

The Carltons' 200-acre homestead included 71 feet of limestone falls. Shown from left to right in 1951 are (front row) James and Miriam Marie Carlton; (second row) Peggy Carlton; her mother, Ellen Marie Crawford Carlton; and Marjorie Lee Carlton. (Courtesy of Marjorie Carlton Simons.)

Pictured from left to right are Margie Lee, James Preston, and Miriam Marie (Peggy) Carlton, children of Johnnie James (J. J.) and Ellen Marie Crawford Carlton. James is known to praise his mother's creative abilities in dyeing fabric from native plants and collects rocks from every county in Texas. (Courtesy of Marjorie Carlton Simons.)

Benjamin Thomas "Doc" Crumley, who often wore a cowboy hat with a turkey feather, was a doctor on the North Shore known for his vast medical knowledge. While living with his Cherokee grandparents for seven years, he learned Native American medicines. Later he attended the highly respected College of William and Mary and then gained further training in France. He was a distinguished Confederate doctor in the Civil War. Crumley is pictured at age 57 in 1879 with his third wife, Lula, age 18. She was the mother of three of Crumley's children. People like Melvina (below, picking cotton) and Albert Lohmann (below and opposite, working the soil) were eternally grateful for Doc's adept and caring ways. (Left, courtesy of Martha Crumley Smalley; below, courtesy of Margaret Lohmann Holloway.)

Three

HARD OLD LAND

The rich, flat soil near the edge of the Colorado River was treasured. Covered wagons crossed the Colorado River and traveled to the Bee Cave's farmers' market outside of Austin. Trips lasted three days—two to travel and one to trade. Campfire evenings held a festive atmosphere filled with visiting and singing. Lohmann's Crossing allowed North Shore families to visit and renew friendships. (Courtesy of Genevieve Kercheville.)

Local beauty Minna "Minnie" Anderson was a feisty, horse-riding postmistress to the North Shore who charmed Harvey Hensel. As Mrs. Hensel, she blessed the North Shore with Pioneer Memorial Cemetery, Hensel Christian Youth Camp, and many festive parties in her cut-rock two-story home surrounded by prized flower gardens. (Courtesy of Joe Kimbro and the Anderson Mill Garden Club.)

James Madison Briggs (1812–1893), his wife, and four children came to Texas and settled close to Austin on Walnut Creek. At the age of 60 in 1872, he filed for a preliminary grant of 160 acres along Cherry Hollow Creek, and he received title to the property in 1877. He and his family were skilled masons and built a 14-foot-by-20-foot rock cabin. Nearby, Briggs dug a 14-foot-deep well, which he lined with rocks. Today the well still contains water at a depth of 8 feet. (Courtesy of Genevieve Kercheville.)

A retired covered wagon frame sits boldly along FM 1431 in 2008, a reminder of frontier days. Covered wagons were used commonly in the area into the 1940s. Wheel marks and frontier ways are permanently carved into North Shore's landscape. (Courtesy of North Shore Heritage and Cultural Society.)

Dillard Singleton and Ollie Phillips drove their horse and buggy to a beautiful setting in a canyon on Spanish Oak Creek. They met a friend and "Preacher" Mobley and were married on the road near Smithwick. That evening, neighbors and friends had a great time when they came to "shivaree" the new couple with bells, things to bang on to make lots of noise, and plans to capture the groom and carry him away. Fortunately, Dillard and Ollie knew what was happening and escaped before Dillard could be captured. (Courtesy of the Singleton family.)

The Lower Colorado River Authority (LCRA) brush cutters were attempting to remove the trees from what would soon be the lake bottom. The Carlton family sadly watched the large tree by their well be cut down. The waters of Lake Travis covered the homestead in September 1940. Rich soil and homesteads were destroyed. Years of work and toil were washed away as the lake covered their homesteads. Homesteaders received only a small amount of money as compensation. (Courtesy of Carlton Family History, Marjorie Carlton Simons.)

In 1927, from left to right, Ethel Maynard, Grace Preece, Clara Vee Maynard, and Margie Turner posed in front of the Maynard house in what was called "Charcoal City." This location on Nameless Road is where they made charcoal. To make charcoal, a large pit was dug, lined with leaves, filled with wood, set afire, and then covered. The hole remained covered for 7 to 10 days. The charcoal was later bagged and sold. (Courtesy of Martha Crumley Smalley.)

James "Phillips" Singleton is pictured with a buck killed on Singleton Ranch in the Travis Peak community in the 1940s. The back porch shows home appliances and a rugged lifestyle. (Courtesy of Ethel Garrett Singleton.)

Bill Pickett (1871–1932) is widely known as the man who invented bulldogging, a method of steer wrestling. In his unconventional technique, he was known even to use his teeth. His family settled at Jenks Branch, located between Liberty Hill and Leander, after emancipation. He broke horses and rode the Chisholm Trail with J. F. Carlton. He also took part in rodeos and a Wild West Show. He is pictured, seated on the right, with his two brothers in the 1890s. (Courtesy of University of Oklahoma Press.)

In the late 1800s, most of the land that later became the Sunset Ranch was not settled or fenced. Many locals would join together for hunts using rifles, horses, and hounds. The Masons had a cabin they used for hunting by Turnback Canyon at the Colorado River. (Both, courtesy of Karen R. Thompson)

The view from the sunset deck at the BCNWR captures the beautiful North Shore Hills, once filled with game for the early settlers. (Courtesy of Karen Kilfeather.)

The Carltons proudly show off their deer hanging near the well at the old J. F. Carlton homestead in the 1940s. From left to right, Essie Mae and J. J. Carlton, an unidentified friend, Leslie and Mona Carlton, and (in front) the two little sons of Leslie and Mona look forward to some venison. The Carltons were known as adept hunters. (Courtesy of Marjorie Carlton Simons.)

One of the North Shore's early land grant settlers, the Pearson family were well known as entrepreneurs. They once owned the lands surrounding and including the Point Venture area. Cattle and goat ranching, a dipping vat, and one of the first gas stations and grocery stores are just a few of their successful businesses. The family continues to own land on the North Shore. Dink and Ivean Pearson were strong community supporters and leaders. (Both, courtesy of the Pearson family.)

Transportation rapidly changed from horse-drawn covered wagons, boats, and trains to cars and airplanes. A rugged vehicle was needed for the North Shore, where curvy, unimproved gravel and caliche roads were a common hardship. A drive down Cow Creek Road today takes one back in time to cattle ranching, gates to open and close, cattle guards, and dry creek beds or rushing flood waters. All of this captures the hill country of the 1940s. (Both, courtesy of North Shore Heritage and Cultural Society.)

Harvey Powers Hensel, pictured at left, was the grandson of Herman Hensel, who left the gold fields of California in 1868 and settled in the Cow Creek Valley as a wealthy man. Harvey inherited the Hensel Ranch and later married Minna "Minnie" Anderson. (Both, courtesy of the Hollingsworth family.)

A Travis Peak landmark is the Hensel House, constructed by Herman Hensel, the postmaster for Travis Peak in 1876. In 1913, his grandson Harvey and Harvey's wife, Minnie, moved into the house. The Hensel home was used in numerous ways over the years, such as a fort and as a polling location during county elections. While their parents voted, children loved to go up and down the stairs, since this was the only two-story structure in the area. (Courtesy of North Shore Heritage and Cultural Society.)

The Hensels operated a general store and the local post office. Local and not-so-local residents would saddle up their steeds and trot in to pick up the mail. During World War II, several Travis Peak men served overseas in various armed forces. Their wives and loved ones would gather at the post office, and many would spend hours waiting. Oral history says that the mail carrier was usually spotted first by Minnie Hensel's parrot Polly, who would squawk, "Mail time! Mail time!" (Courtesy of North Shore Heritage and Cultural Society.)

This ornamental wrought iron fence surrounds the Hensel Memorial Cemetery, built to honor a pioneer family who died of cholera on the Hensel property as they traveled to the West Texas country. Graves from the late 1800s and early 1900s occupy this small bit of Texas soil. Herman Hensel's headstone stands in the middle of the cemetery and displays the sign of the Freemasons. (Courtesy of North Shore Heritage and Cultural Society.)

In 1965, Minnie Hensel set aside 337 acres of the Hensel Ranch as a Christian encampment facility. There are eight dormitories and a magnificent dining hall that can be used as an auditorium or play area during bad weather. In addition to teaching by Christian men and women, many activities are available. Her wish was that the Hensel Ranch would continue to be available to young and old alike to enjoy fellowship and a renewing of their spirits in the beautiful hill country where she and Harvey spent many happy days with friends and neighbors. (Courtesy of North Shore Heritage and Cultural Society.)

Four

FIRM FOUNDATIONS

Pioneers transformed the land thought to be not appropriate for homesteads into communities along the North Shore. The one-room Fairview School was active from 1870 to 1945. The present building was constructed in 1909. Fairview became the community of Nameless after six names were rejected by the U.S. postal system. The residents responded, "let the community be nameless and be damned." Nameless School celebrated its centennial in 2009. (Courtesy of Genevieve Kercheville.)

Stephen F. Austin's Upper Colony schoolhouses provided the foundation for communities and towns to emerge and flourish. The core of social development along the North Shore of the Colorado River was firmly established within the chain of one-room schoolhouses. Spanish Oaks School, Double Horn School, and Haynie Flat School (shown above) were near Marble Falls. Unfortunately, many of these schools have been moved or destroyed. (Courtesy of LCRA.)

Easter Lily Wade Whitt, who taught at Round Mountain School from 1937 to 1941, shared her memories of "the favorite time in her life" at the age of 90. She spoke to the Lake Travis Extension Education Association at Nameless School. Easter taught grades one through eight at the one-room school with an abundance of love and precision. Her vivid recall brings an understanding of the mastery of the pioneer teachers. (Courtesy of North Shore Heritage and Cultural Society.)

Cox Springs School, once located on Sylvester Road, was near the vital Lohmann's Crossing. The Pearson family's children were students from the school's inception until the 1940s. A photograph taken in the 1920s shows Ivean Pearson, who is the tall boy in front of the window. The second boy to the left of Ivean is brother Wesley. The boy in the sailor shirt is his brother Scoot, and the second girl to the right of him is his sister Hazel. (Courtesy of Claretta Pearson England.)

Dink Pearson Park marks Lohmann's Crossing near the village of Point Venture. Unlike most of the original land grant families who sold their land, the Pearson family continues to own theirs. Documents show Ed Pearson purchased 320 acres of land from the Texas School Land Fund in 1905 for $1.25 an acre. A proof of occupancy and improvements document states that required improvements were completed by 1906 for a total of $330. (Courtesy of North Shore Heritage and Cultural Society.)

Round Mountain School is located in the Sandy Creek area 7 miles from Leander. It was started in a log cabin on land donated by Jesse Smith and J. R. Faubion in the 1870s. The dedicated community improved its schoolhouse in 1888, when a new wooden structure was built. Unfortunately, the 1888 building and its 1929 replacement were both destroyed by fire. The present school building was built in 1935 and is currently being refurbished. It remains a vital community center. (Courtesy of North Shore Heritage and Cultural Society.)

Members of the Lake Travis Extension Education Association stand proudly in front of Nameless School in its restored state. The association has held weekly quilting sessions and monthly meetings in Nameless School for the last 50 years. The association achieved its goal of the school restoration in time for its centennial in 2009 through the use of grants, donations, quilt raffles, history and cookbook sales, and other fund-raisers. Nameless community members continued in the North Shore pioneer spirit by assisting in the physical labor needed to complete the restoration. (Courtesy of Genevieve Kercheville.)

The Rock School House was attended by Travis Peak families. It sits on part of the Hensel Christian Youth Camp. Its perfectly constructed masonry stands as a tribute to excellent construction skills. (Courtesy of North Shore Heritage and Cultural Society.)

The Travis Peak School II was a wood structure moved from Turkey Bend in 1872 by William H. H. Singleton. It was located on the Turner Ranch, just south of the Dillard Singleton property, on a 35-yard-by-35-yard square piece of land located next to "the 5 acres that is to encompass the church and cemetery for use as a school" donated by Elizabeth "Aunt Bet" Singleton. The 1938 class shown here is, from left to right, Mary Lou Singleton, Hugh Singleton, Martin Leon Blessing, Virginia Onita Singleton, Erby Garrett, Stanley Singleton, Nona Fay Hall, and Foy Phelan. (Courtesy of the Singleton family.)

Richard Rodgers (1868–1922) was born in County Down, Northern Ireland. At the age of 14, he left his home and traveled to Australia, Canada, Chicago, and finally Houston in 1895. He started a small grocery store in Houston with $400 and then went on to invest in rooming houses and hotels. He later entered into real estate and organized the Sunset Realty Company. In 1911, he greatly changed the face of the North Shore when he bought a 22,000-acre ranch in western Travis County and named it the Sunset Ranch. The Rodgers family continues to live on part of the ranch and are avid supporters of the community. (Courtesy of the Rodgers family.)

Blanche Genevieve Klotz (1883–1968) married Richard Rodgers in Houston in 1901, when she was 18 and he was 32. At Blanche's insistence, the Sunset ranch house was built in 1911 with indoor plumbing, the first house in the area to have such a convenience. They raised five children. (Courtesy of the Rodgers family.)

When Richard Rodgers and his family arrived from Houston by train, they were met in Leander by a horse-drawn wagon to take them to the ranch house he had built off Nameless Road. The original entrance gate is on Nameless Road near Leander. Two additional black gates can be seen along FM 1431 on the way to Marble Falls. (Courtesy of North Shore Heritage and Cultural Society.)

Rodgers family members in this 1940 photograph are, from left to right, Richard Jr., Marion, Blanche Genevieve, George Hamilton, Dorothy Genevieve, and James. All the Rodgers children spent their early years in Houston, but they and their descendants have enjoyed living on the ranch in recent times. (Courtesy of the Rodgers family.)

Sunset Ranch is symbolic of the enduring, adventurous spirit throughout the North Shore. Flashes of history recall the wildcatters' search for black gold in 1919. Even though oil was not found, many treasures were yet to be discovered in this cattle country: meteorites, endangered species, hunting opportunities, and vacation vistas. (Courtesy of Genevieve Kercheville.)

Water and lack of water were constant threats. Flooding washed away crops one season and drought left the lands parched the next. Homesteaders not located near the shores of the Colorado River faced even graver conditions as they fought against the rocky terrain. Bodies of men and women alike became deformed from carrying water, digging wells, and constructing cisterns. Remains of their hand-dug wells and hand-built cisterns demonstrate excellent construction skills and endurance. Both deserve admiration. Windmills in pioneer Texas were primarily for pumping water for livestock and farm and home needs. The windmill above still remains on the Hensel property. The water cistern to the right, built by the Maynard family, is located in Jonestown behind the historic Carter Jones Realty offices and demonstrates the remarkable construction skills of the pioneers. The cistern is famous for its yearly attraction of chimney swifts, an event registered with the Audubon Society. (Both, courtesy of North Shore Heritage and Cultural Society.)

Rich memories were formed from handmade treasures, such as this quilt hand-crafted by the grandmother of Singleton Bend men Mose (left) and Dillard Singleton (right). The times required a different way of life, such as the innovation of the zip line (below) located on the Colley Ranch to cross Sandy Creek when flooding occurred. Inventive results solved problems and brought comfort. (Above, courtesy of the Singleton family; below, courtesy of Barbara Dugone.)

Around 1931, a 20-span concrete bridge known as "Lohmann's Bridge," which connected the North Shore with what is now the Lakeway area, was paid for by local residents. The contractor was C. A. Manfrais, the first cement company in the Austin area. After the bridge was completed at a cost of $4,000, a community dinner and dance was held in the middle of the bridge. Ivean Pearson provided a barbecue cow. This bridge is now under the waters of Lake Travis, as is the Lohmann homestead. John Henry Lohmann (1799–1891) came to Texas with his wife and four children from Hanover, Germany, in 1942. He first settled in an area where the University of Texas is now located and established a dairy with 11 cows. The dairy provided all of the milk for the city of Austin. Because of his opposition to secession, in 1861, he moved with his second wife and family to a piece of property on the South Shore of the then-Colorado River, where he built a large stone house and five tenant cabins. Because of his large family, the Lohmann name is very prominent in the North Shore and South Shore of Lake Travis. (Courtesy of the Pearson family.)

Homesteaders were joined by a new type of wealthy, adventurous settler. The Sylvester family sold riverfront property perched high upon the cliffs of Arkansas Bend to Dr. Denton Cooley, a respected heart surgeon from Houston. Many of his famous associates visited his retreat, shown above. The property is now part of Dr. David and Leslie Winn's ranch. (Courtesy of North Shore Heritage and Cultural Society.)

After graduating from the University of Texas in 1935, George H. "Buddy" Rodgers began his lifetime work of managing his family's Sunset Ranch. By 1940, he had built a home and married Margaret Schirmer. These former Houstonians felt like pioneers as they began to raise a family on the ranch. With no electricity and little insulation in the homes, many found the shade of the canopy of live oak trees and porches cooler than inside the homes. (Courtesy of the Rodgers family.)

In 1939, Gilbert and his brother Bruce
Ballerstedt enjoyed climbing the
hill country cliff at Arkansas Bend.
These rock formations now are hidden
under Lake Travis. Gilbert, a film
projectionist in Austin, purchased
the land from the Denton Cooley
family. His passion for building and
for retreating to his fishing camp is
evident in his photography archives.
(Courtesy of the Ballerstedt family.)

Rose "Bunce" Maude, Gilbert Ballerstedt's
wife, sets a daring stance as she stands
in front of the Colorado River near the
Ballerstedts' fishing lodge. A modern
lodge that includes cherished parts
of the original camp continues to be
used often by Ballerstedt's descendants,
the Red and Rose Olander family.
(Courtesy of the Ballerstedt family.)

Gilbert, Bunce, and their daughter Rose Ballestedt would use their boat *Gillie* in 1943 to cross the Colorado River (later Lake Travis) to enjoy their Shangri Lodge at Arkansas Bend. (Courtesy of the Ballerstedt family.)

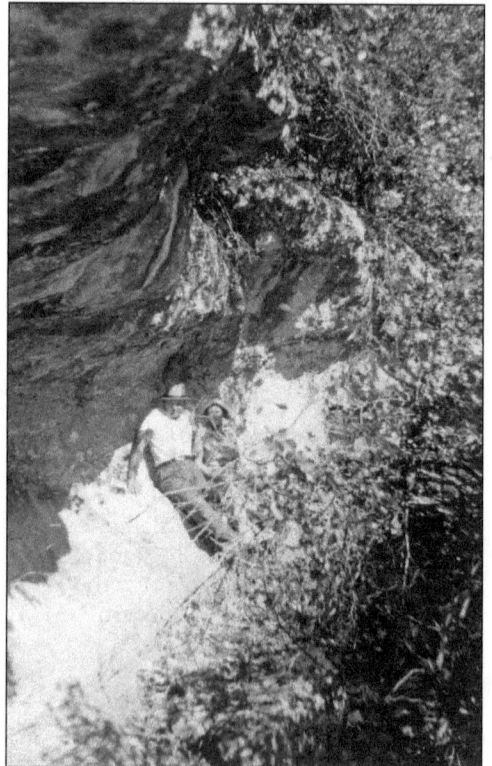

Hanging Rock Springs was known as a place of shelter and pure spring water for early travelers. Pictured here are Marian and Frank Webster in the 1940s. Originally situated on Sunset Ranch, this tract of land became part of the Balcones Canyonland National Wildlife Refuge in the 1990s. (Courtesy of the Rodgers family.)

Five

Shock Waves

As North Shore landowners looked at the massive dam built at Marshall's Ford, they saw both opportunity and disaster. Families' dreams, homes, cemeteries, rich bottomland orchards, and gardens were threatened. Sources for financial stability no longer existed. The proceeds from the forced sales of their land were inadequate. Opportunities once available by crossing the river were now miles away. (Courtesy of the Rodgers family.)

In 1941, the name of Marshall Ford Dam was changed to Mansfield Dam in honor of Congressman J. J. Mansfield. Lake Travis, a flood control lake, began to form behind the massive dam. Mansfield Dam is 279 feet high, 7,089 feet long, and 213 feet thick at the base. Water storage capability in the lake reaches 369 billion gallons, and hydroelectric power is generated. The promise Lyndon Baines Johnson had made to bring electric power to the North Shore was realized in the 1950s. (Courtesy of Karen Kilfeather.)

The North Shore of Lake Travis became an attraction for visitors seeking to purchase land on Lake Travis. The Bar-K airstrip had numerous planes landing daily with families hoping to own a lake home being sold by farmers and ranchers facing financial crisis. (Courtesy of World of Resorts.)

Lake Travis became a thriving waterway for boats hauling loads of rock or other goods. It was a quicker route for transportation than travel over caliche roads. (Courtesy of the Ballerstedt family.)

Warren and Lura Jones initiated the first stages of recreational development on the North Shore in 1939. Warren was one of the Jones brothers who founded Jonestown. Warren and Lura purchased the Frank Maynard ranch house, known as the first house in Jonestown, and are pictured below entering their home. The house is now the Jones and Carter Realtors office. (Courtesy of the Jones family.)

As a high school student, Betty Jo Carter stands on the lot where her daughter, Donna, would build her home years later. The Sandy Creek arm of Lake Travis is in the background. When her father, Warren Jones, bought 300 acres of land in 1935, they did not know the lake was coming. While Mansfield Dam was being constructed, LCRA decided to raise the height of the dam due to a flood that almost destroyed Austin. When the level of the dam was raised, the water came up Sandy Creek, creating a beautiful arm of Lake Travis. (Courtesy of the Jones family.)

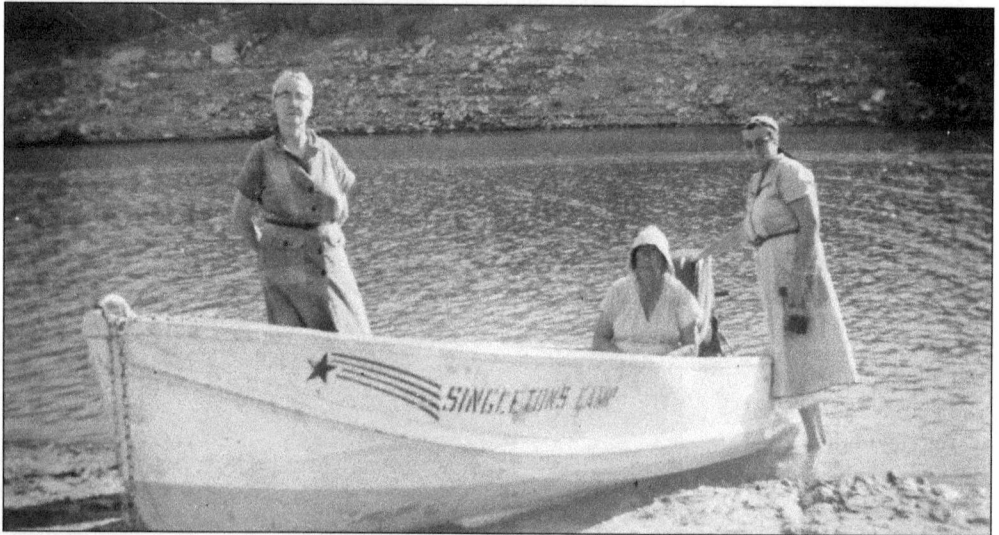

Soon after Lake Travis was created by the construction of Mansfield Dam, quick-thinking Dillard and Ollie Singleton of Travis Peak bought seven boats to rent out to fishermen. Later Dillard and his son-in-law, G. W. Wood, built a rock cabin to rent by the day or week. Several people built cabins on land they rented from the Singletons. The fishing camp not only provided income, but Ollie loved talking and visiting with the people who came to fish and camp. Pictured here are three Singleton ladies: Ollie (in bonnet), Sudie (left), and Penny. (Courtesy of the Singleton family.)

56

In the midst of the rapid change of the 1940s, folks like the Rodgers family found their favorite swimming holes just as refreshing as new swimming pools. (Courtesy of the Rodgers family.)

Fishing cabins and retreats became a popular way of life in the 1930s. Wading down the creek was a favorite pastime for the second-home residents. (Courtesy of the Ballerstedt family.)

Sons of North Shore joined the military to make a difference in the world's future during World War II. S.Sgt. Vernon Hollingsworth (left) resigned from his teaching job to serve in the 360th Air Service Squadron, where he was a bomb sight specialist. James "Phillips" Singleton (below) was a telegraph operator in the 147th Armored Signal Company. As a telegraph operator, he was one of the first to receive the message that President Roosevelt had died. Curley Simpson served as a bulldozer operator. Hugh Singleton, a medic in the infantry, received two purple hearts. Each veteran's service and dedication added to victory and world peace. (Left, courtesy of the Hollingworth family; below, courtesy of the Singleton family.)

The city of Jonestown on the North Shore is the site of Jonestown Veterans Memorial Park by Jim and Shelby Thomas. In that park, the Going Home veterans plaque and statue of a soldier combine to make a statement of appreciation. Our veterans' stories became one—brave men and women giving their lives to protect others. The inscription reads: "Throughout our nation's history, our armed forces have served in conflicts and returned. This reflective memorial is dedicated by VFW Hill Country Post # 6795 and the City of Jonestown in the spring of 2003." Veterans from around the world have chosen the North Shore as their home. (Courtesy of North Shore Heritage and Cultural Society.)

An aerial view of the North Shore reveals how the hill country and Lake Travis combined to make a beautiful setting for adventure and vacations. Sid Wheless was first to establish an extensive fishing lodge. Newt Johnson, a Houston restaurateur, was next on the scene and expanded it to the Bar-K Guest Ranch. (Courtesy of the Johnson family.)

In 1980, the Sunset Ranch was divided into five separate ranches for the five Rodgers siblings. Buddy Rodgers had been running cattle over the entire ranch for more than 40 years. With less acreage to use, he sold many of the cattle. For the first time, he had a manageable herd to brand and work. (Courtesy of the Rodgers family.)

Six

RECREATION PARADISE

As the dinner bell rang, guests headed toward the Bar-K Club House in the 1950s. A world-famous chef and exceptional dining waited as well as a full range of activities to fill their agendas. Local people enjoyed working at the Bar-K Guest Ranch. Newt and Liz Johnson's son Tom, often called "Mayor," shared the duties of managing the ranch. (Courtesy of the Johnson family.)

A popular gas station and store was frequently used by Bar-K guests, hunters, and fishing parties while visiting the North Shore in the 1950s. (Courtesy of the Jones family.)

Wild grasses, horses, and airplanes began to symbolize the North Shore. The creatively decorated red Bar-K van could be seen picking up guests who flew into the Bar-K airstrip. Luggage and vacationers were transported to the ranch. Brave vacationers could travel back to the clubhouse and view the beautiful countryside on horseback. (Courtesy of the Johnson family.)

In 1958, Astronaut Alan Sheppard (right) is pictured with Chuck Johnson. Chuck was the son of Tom and Faye Johnson and the first child born in the area now called Lago Vista. Alan was visiting Dr. Paul Harris, the visionary developer of Lago Vista. (Courtesy of the Johnson family.)

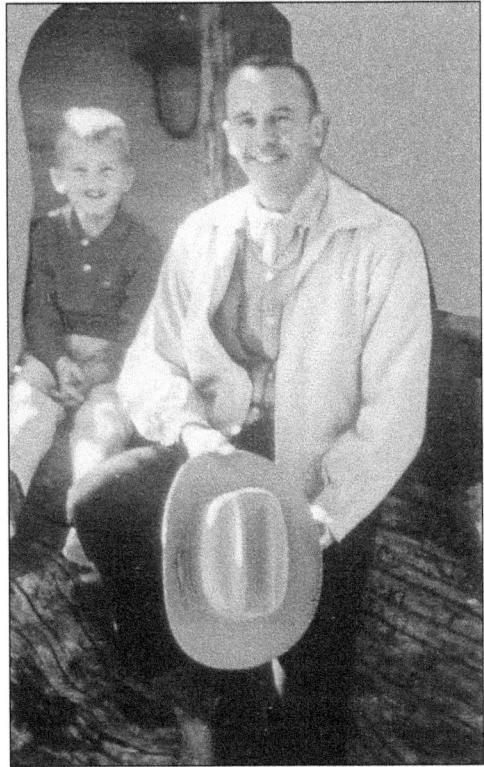

Newt and Liz Johnson purchased the first residential home constructed in Lago Vista. The home remains in the Johnson family. Robin Burkhart, the current owner, is the daughter of Elgin and Jennifer (Johnson) Faulkner and the granddaughter of Newt and Liz Johnson. The home is located near the Bar-K on Dawn Drive and displays the first awarded historical marker. Pictured from left to right are Guy and Robin Burkhart, Tom and Faye Johnson, Jennifer Johnson Faulkner and Elgin Faulkner, and Rachel Tomlinson and Lynae Mann, granddaughters of Newt and Liz Johnson. (Courtesy of Shirley Davis.)

Nighttime entertainment included barbecue dinners accompanied by cowboy singers. (Courtesy of the Johnson family.)

Elgin Faulkner, a noted water skiing champion, enjoyed his visits to Lake Travis with his wife, Jennifer Johnson Faulkner. (Courtesy of the Faulkner family.)

In June 1966, nighttime boating on Lake Travis was exciting as Bar-K Ranch's Tom Johnson steered the boat. One of the young couples boating with Tom and his wife Faye were Joel and Cordelia Cummings. The Cummings became part of the development of Point Venture. In 1970, four investors from Houston bought the property, now called Point Venture: S. W. "Woody" Gaylord, Bill Canfield, Joel Cummins, and Lawrence Clayton Smith. (Courtesy of the Johnson family.)

Robert Culp, who played a Texas Ranger in the television series *Trackdown* from 1957 to 1959, was a guest at the Texas Rangers conference held at the Bar-K Guest Ranch. (Courtesy of the Johnson family.)

Horseback riding attracted large groups who loved the days of old Texas. Healthy horses, comfortable saddles, beautiful hillside views, picnic lunches, and fellow riders made the day a fond memory. (Courtesy of the Johnson family.)

Deer have attracted hunters to the hill country from Native American times to the present. Skilled guides, game handlers, warm meals, and a comfortable bed were a few of the benefits when hunting at the Bar-K Guest Ranch. (Courtesy of the Johnson family.)

At the Bar-K Guest Ranch in the 1950s, Betty and Max David Melcher (above) joined the morning Chuck Wagon trail ride, which went up to the top of Cow Mountain. All the "dudes" rode single-file behind the trail boss, Mossy Dedear (below). (Above, courtesy of the Melcher family; below, courtesy of Johnson family.)

The Travis Peak Church of Christ planted and groomed a tree arbor to serve as their first sanctuary. The well-trimmed cluster of trees can be seen in the right back corner of the photograph. Their 100-year-old church building was built in 1909 to house the oldest church on the North Shore. (Courtesy of the Singleton family.)

Convenience stores and mailboxes became common meeting areas. Jonestown's early gas station was used by locals as well as visitors on fishing trips. A Shell station continues to provide services in the same location. (Courtesy of the Jones family.)

Ola (Colley) Donahue, daughter of William and Barbara Colley, is pictured in 1928 demonstrating skill and a risk-taking attitude as she performs on a horse. The Colley Ranch, established in 1879, is marked by its gate on Nameless Road. (Courtesy of Barbara Donahue Dugone.)

Rodeos were an early Fourth of July tradition on the Sunset Ranch for the community. Later inventive goat rodeos with high precision skills provided great fun at the Bar-K Rodeo Show Time. Outdoor movies capped the evening. (Courtesy of the Johnson family.)

Retreats were often held at Bar-K. Sorority girls are pictured here enjoying a cowboy breakfast. Guitar playing and singing added to the weekend. (Courtesy of the Johnson family.)

Nothing was better than leaving Houston in a 1957 Chevy and arriving at Bar-K on Lake Travis. Memories of great fishing highlighted the weekend for Betty Melcher in the 1960s. (Courtesy of the Melcher family.)

Cool, crystal waters enticed Texans to become boat owners. High-powered motorboats became the rage as boaters cruised Lake Travis. At right, boating and fishing was known to put smiles on the faces of twins Jeff (left) and Phil Johnson (right). (Both, courtesy of the Johnson family.)

Gilbert and Bunce Ballerstedt's daughter Rose Marie and her friend Cecil Rennerly visited Lake Travis from Austin in 1941. The girls were enchanted by the endless beauty of Lake Travis as it rose at Arkansas Bend. (Courtesy of the Ballerstedt family.)

The lake soon became equated with beauty and fun. Pontoon boats provided space for small groups to enjoy an afternoon of fun and sun as they leisurely traveled the lake. Swimming, fishing, music, and picnics were enjoyed by many. (Courtesy of the Johnson family.)

Horseback riding was one of the favorite activities at the Bar-K Guest Ranch. Riders, who ranged from movie stars to real rangers, enjoyed the Bar-K paradise. (Courtesy of the Johnson family.)

Beulah Christine (Lewis) Hollingsworth celebrated her 100th birthday with a party at the home of her granddaughter, Saundra (Hollingsworth) Howard. In the picture, Sherry (Allison) Shewmaker, Beulah's great-granddaughter, presents her with a presidential recognition certificate from George H. Bush. In 1922, Beulah and her husband, Otho Edwin Hollingsworth, bought 320 acres along the Colorado River in the area now known as Gloster Bend. They farmed cotton, corn, and maize and also gathered pecans as a cash crop. (Courtesy of the Hollingsworth family.)

A Jonestown Girl Scout group enjoys wading in the water flowing over a dam on Brushy Creek. (Courtesy of the Jones family.)

A snowfall in the mid-1940s provides fun for Otho Hollingsworth, his daughter-in-law Jean (Shepard) Hollingsworth, granddaughter Janice, and the family dog, Jack. Their home, shown in the background, was built from native stone removed from the banks of the Colorado River before it became Lake Travis. This unique rock work home still remains on the Hollingsworth farm. (Courtesy of the Hollingsworth family.)

Seven

RESORTS TO
RETIREMENT HAVEN

With the completion of the dam at Marshall Ford (later named Mansfield Dam), the narrow and undependable Colorado River became Lake Travis in 1941 and forever changed the face of the North Shore. In spite of the curvy and narrow caliche roads, visitors who arrived as guests at Jones's fishing camps were eager to become property owners. Land developers discovered Lake Travis's lure of crystal blue water, good fishing, and inviting vistas. (Courtesy of the Jones family.)

Signs of early communities remain on marked roads. Sylvester Ford and Singleton Bend, like many roads, took the names of early landowners and referenced their positions on the Colorado River. Cedar poles with wooden nameplates appeared, as well as signs listing area residents and the estimated miles to their homes. As mail service advanced, rows of attached mailboxes at main intersections became common sights. (Courtesy of North Shore Heritage and Cultural Society.)

In 1958, Houston dentist C. Paul Harris purchased 6,000 acres from retired war hero Sid Wheless and established Lago Vista Estates, Inc. Harris's successful El Lago home development project near Nassau Bay attracted Houston buyers. Families from Houston quickly purchased land, and homes followed. As the population grew, schools were impacted. To alleviate the situation, Dr. Harris donated a building on Lohmann Road for the Little Red School House. (Courtesy of North Shore Heritage and Cultural Society.)

"Greetings from Lago Vista!" continues to represent the welcoming attitude of North Shore. Entrepreneurs were welcomed. George Marshall bought 1,800 acres of land on Lake Travis in 1945. From Hatter's Cove to Devil's Hollow, he established his breathtaking Lakeshore Ranch. It remains a favorite subdivision. George Marshall, Sid Wheless, and Emmett Jones made the deal with Stormy Davis of Southwestern Bell for phone service in October 1959. Local government, property owners associations, and fire departments were manned by volunteers. Selfless volunteers built libraries and other organizations. (Courtesy of Vasara Photography.)

The Lago Vista Volunteer Fire Department (LVVFD) was an important element in the successful progress of the North Shore area. At the 10th anniversary of the department, the volunteers who had worked to establish it, A. W. "Shorty" Ludwick (left) and his wife, "Snooks" Ludwick (middle), were honored with a plaque commemorating the occasion. Ben Templin (right), president of the LVVFD Board of Fire Commissioners, presented the plaque. (Courtesy of the Van Cleave family.)

The small airstrip built by Sid Wheless to make travel more accessible to his Bar-K fishing camp soon became a key ingredient in the development of the North Shore. The Bar-K Airport Developers oversaw its growth until 1986. Later Japanese developer Taiyo Corporation became the owners of the North Shore's three golf courses and also spent over $100,000 to pave the airport runway in 1989. (Courtesy of World of Resorts.)

National Resort Communities employed pilots at the Bar-K airstrip. The Southwest Federal Aviation Agency recognized, from left to right, Jim Ewen, Bo Laughterbach, and Sterling Costlow for their abilities and conscientiousness in 1972 by awarding them the Operation of the Year Award. (Courtesy of National Resorts Communities.)

As one of the early leaders of the City of Lago Vista, Rusty Allen served as a mayor and worked to develop the Lago Vista airport and the Rusty Allen Air Power Museum. (Above, courtesy of the Rusty Allen family; below, courtesy of the North Shore Heritage and Cultural Society.)

Lago Vista Golf Course (LVGC) opened in 1975. Under the ownership of National Resort International, Inc., members of the club enjoyed a full schedule of social activities such as golf, tennis, swimming, cards, and fine dining. (Courtesy of World of Resorts.)

Orville Moody, also known as "Sarge," was the professional golfer on staff at LVGC in the 1970s. He lived near the golf course at 998 Outpost Trace until a fire destroyed his house. He had become a passionate professional golfer after completing his military service and won the U.S. Open in 1972 while working at LVGC. (Courtesy of World of Resorts.)

The 18-hole Lago Vista Country Club was dedicated before a crowd of 7,000 people who had come to witness the realization of a dream. The dedication took place on a sunny, moderately warm golf day with crystal-clear skies. (Courtesy of World of Resorts.)

Golfer Lee Trevino was a big hit in Lago Vista. He was one of the sport's top money winners and a crowd pleaser with his excellent golfing skills and playful personality. (Courtesy of World of Resorts.)

Zach Padgett, the current manager and professional golf teacher at Lago Vista City Golf Course, has an interesting history with the North Shore. As a four-year golf team member at the University of Texas, Zach often practiced and fine-tuned his game on Lago Vista's golf courses. After graduating college in 1970, Zach became a PGA Class A golfer. His first position as a golf instructor and head pro was at the Lago Vista Golf Course from 1974 to 1979. Welcome back, Zach. (Courtesy of the Padgett family.)

Point Venture Golf Course opened in 1972 and is a nine-hole course located in a hill country setting. Director Justin Orbin was voted one of America's best golf instructors. Another local nine-hole course is the Bar-K Golf Course, known for its challenging putting greens. (Courtesy of North Shore Heritage and Cultural Society.)

Chris Shive, driving on a LVGC tee in 2009, marks the pose of a skilled golfer as he participates in a local fund-raising tournament. The World of Resort Condominium Community Men's Golf Association was formed in 1983. Many individuals enjoy the Lago Vista Golf Course. (Courtesy of *North Lake Travis LOG*.)

In 1994, a visiting Sony executive discovered soon-to-be-famous Rick Trevino singing at a local restaurant, the Thirsty Turtle, which was owned by Bob and Jean Mroski. The popular Hispanic singer remains well-known in the country music world for singing "Honky Tonk Crowd" and other songs. (Courtesy of the Mroski family.)

The Travis Peak Church of Christ sanctuary was built in 1909. It has remained an active church for 100 years, with many of the frontier descendants making up the congregation that attended Sunday services in brush arbors and other buildings near this site. (Courtesy of North Shore Heritage and Cultural Society.)

The elegant St. Peter's Episcopal Church is in a beautiful white sandstone building with an adjacent activity center. It is nestled into a magnificent setting overlooking Lake Travis. It has many breathtaking outdoor worship areas. (Courtesy of North Shore Heritage and Cultural Society.)

Rolling Hills Community Church's ground-breaking ceremony was in 1981. (Courtesy of Rolling Hills Community Church.)

The original sign for the Rolling Hills Community Church marks the location where members built a multidenominational church. The church expanded to three buildings to accommodate their extensive range of ministries. (Courtesy of Rolling Hills Community Church.)

This building was the meeting place for community organizations. Four villages formed and then met individually to address local issues: Lago Vista Country Club, Highland Lakes Estates, Highland Country Club, and Bar-K. The building accommodated many other types of meetings. The first mass of St. Mary's Catholic Church was held on December 6, 1970. (Courtesy of St. Mary's Catholic Church.)

St. Mary's Catholic Church has grown into one of the largest churches on the North Shore. Metal sculptures, stained glass windows, and other beautiful art adorns the church. Msgr. Joseph Schmidt, more commonly known as Father Joe, has been the priest there since 1970. He was born and raised on the North Shore. (Courtesy of St. Mary's Catholic Church.)

The Jonestown Church of Christ began in 1946. Their first worship services were held in the afternoon at Cox Springs School once located on Lohmann Road, and they shared a minister with a neighboring church. Descendants of early North Shore settlers built their current church building in 1968. They continue to welcome new members. (Courtesy of North Shore Heritage and Cultural Society.)

Christ Our Savior Lutheran Church was dedicated in February 1988 and is located on FM 1431. It is marked with three prominent crosses, which are decorated to celebrate religious holidays. (Courtesy of North Shore Heritage and Cultural Society.)

The Travis Oaks Baptist Church held its first services in a tent. The first church was constructed in 1972. (Courtesy of Travis Oaks Baptist Church.)

Several additions have been made to the Travis Oaks Baptist Church to accommodate growth. The beautiful building on Boggy Ford Road provides church services and numerous educational programs for all age groups. (Courtesy of North Shore Heritage and Cultural Society.)

The First Baptist Church of Jonestown was established in the mid-1960s. The sanctuary on FM 1431 is situated in a park-like setting. In April 2009, the church began to diversify its ministry by having two Sunday worship services—one in English and one in Spanish. (Courtesy of North Shore Heritage and Cultural Society.)

The North Shore has many churches and religious organizations, including the United Christian Scientist Reading Room, First Church of Christ, Hill Country Bible Church, and North Lake Bible Church. In addition, services and educational programs are held at homes, schools, community buildings, and outdoors. Meet You at the Pole, a youth service held at Lago Vista Middle School, is an example of exciting religious events not in local churches. Chris Moseley plays the guitar as students gather around in 2008. (Courtesy of North Lake Travis LOG.)

The Island, built on Lake Travis in 1988, has many beautiful lakeside villas. However, Lake Travis is a flood control lake, with drastic fluctuations in water levels that affect waterfront properties. The levels of Lake Travis created an unusual landscape for The Island during a drought on October 1, 2009. The lake level was at its lowest in over 50 years. (Courtesy of *North Lake Travis LOG*.)

Flooding creates an equally unusual landscape at the Bar-K clubhouse, which was built in the 1950s. (Courtesy of *North Lake Travis LOG*.)

90

Eight

ANNEXATION? NO WAY!

The City of Austin, seeing endless, rich possibilities, had hopeful intentions to annex the area and gain valuable water rights. Annexation attempts were abruptly halted when three independent-minded communities became independent governing bodies. Each community continues to support recreational activities with special emphasis on Lake Travis. The climate and beautiful vistas attract golfers to four golf courses. Social, educational, and religious gatherings continue to offer an array of opportunities. (Courtesy of North Shore Heritage and Cultural Society.)

MAYOR SAM BILLINGS

It was just a few years before World War II that the community of Jonestown began to take shape. Originally settled in the 1930s, Jonestown was established as a hunting and fishing community in 1939 by Warren and Emmett Jones. The Jonestown community was once reluctant to become a city, but it is now a thriving one. Deane Armstrong welcomes Texas state dignitaries to her mayoral swearing-in ceremony. Deane was elected mayor once again in 2008. (Courtesy of the Van Cleave family.)

The event of the year on Lake Travis is the Fourth of July celebration. People, businesses, floats, and boats can be seen everywhere, dressed and decorated in red, white, and blue, with flags waving. Nighttime fireworks delight the evening crowds. One of Jonestown's early mayors was Sam Billings, a descendant of Emmett Jones. Sam dons an all-American hat to celebrate the Fourth of July. (Courtesy of the City of Jonestown.)

The city of Jonestown celebrated October Fest in 2008. Jones Brothers Park on Lake Travis sparkled with people nestled under ancient oak trees to enjoy music, art, food, drinks, and visitors, from the original Hornsby family who settled Travis County to newly arrived hill country residents. Artists' booths displayed quality original creations at affordable prices. (Courtesy of North Shore Heritage and Cultural Society.)

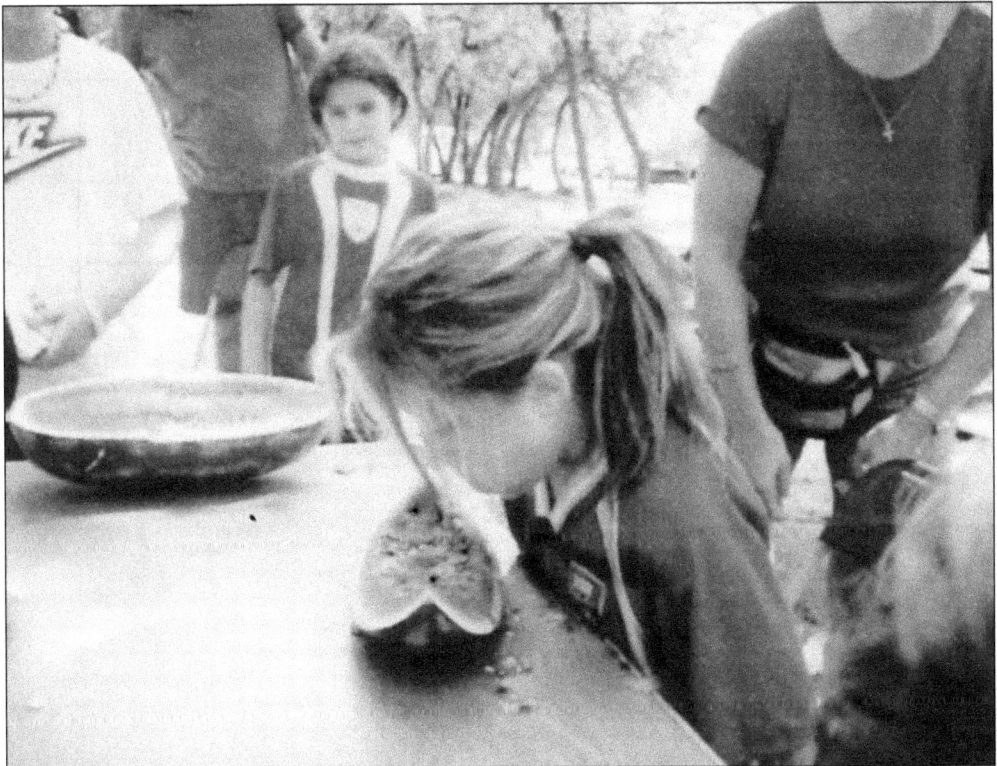

Lago Vista's Hill Country Dayz Festival sponsored by the Lago Vista Chamber of Commerce has become a prized event on the North Shore. An abundance of music, food, arts and crafts draw festive community participants. Adults and children alike are provided with fun and adventure at the Bar-K Park. The watermelon-eating contest and many other attractions provide fun and accent the hill country theme. (Courtesy of *North Lake Travis LOG*.)

The Lago Vista city entry sign on the corner of Lohmann's Road and FM 1431 marks the path to the main part of the city. It is situated in front of a rapidly growing modern shopping mall and was financed by members of the community. CVS Pharmacy was the first business to open in 2007. (Courtesy of North Shore Heritage and Cultural Society.)

No local newspaper existed until around 1981, when Bob Freer established the *Beacon*. C. D. and Gloria Van Cleave later established the *North Lake Travis LOG* and published the first edition in February 1982. In June 1988, the Tooley family bought the newspaper and published it for several years. It is now owned by Cox Newspapers' subsidiary, Austin Community Newspapers, and remains a vital part of North Shore life. (Courtesy of the Van Cleave family.)

Lago Vista Post Office, a branch of the Leander Post Office, was built in 2000. It provides a spacious, modern, and convenient facility. (Courtesy of North Shore Heritage and Cultural Society.)

Lago Vista and Jonestown libraries, popular and frequently used facilities, offer activities for all ages ranging from adult computer and writing classes to children's reading programs. Volunteers started the libraries and have continued to play an important role in providing services. The library directors, Marji Smith and Jan Steele, have been instrumental in assisting with research for the writing of this publication. (Courtesy of North Shore Heritage and Cultural Society.)

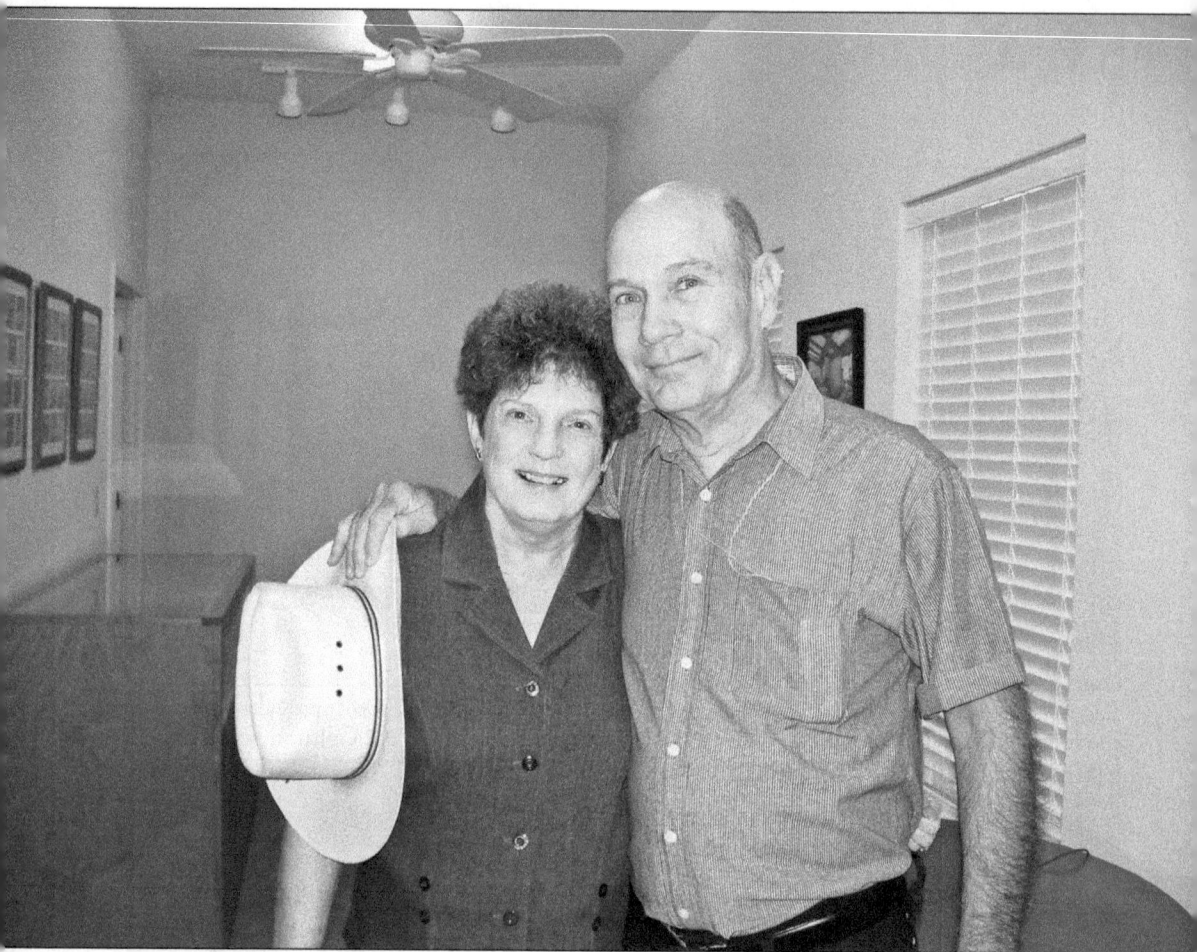

Joe England and Claretta Pearson-England, founding members of the North Shore Heritage and Cultural Society, enjoy sharing the early history of the area now called Point Venture with historians. (Courtesy of North Shore Heritage and Cultural Society.)

Lohmann's Bridge once connected the north and south shores of the Colorado River. Today beautiful homes and a few vacant waterfront lots can be found in this area. In 2009, the going price for a quarter-acre of land was $799,000. In 1859, only 150 years ago, the land sold for little more than 30¢ per quarter-acre. (Courtesy of North Shore Heritage and Cultural Society.)

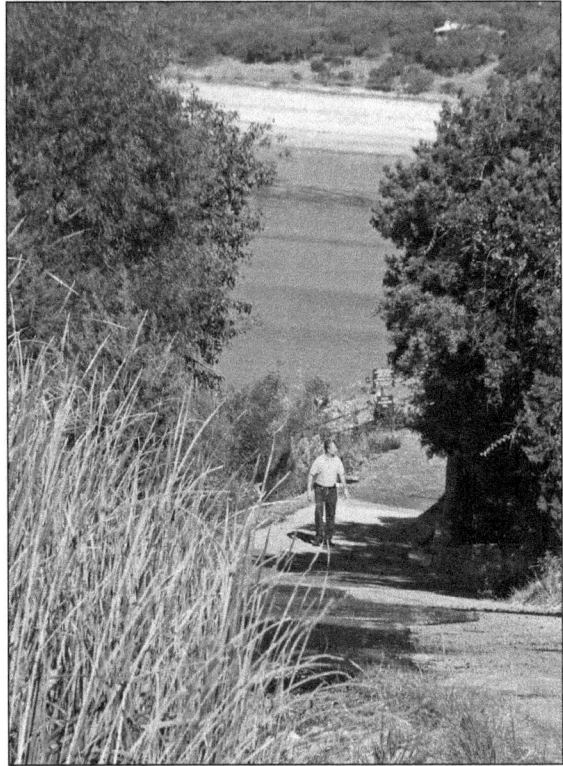

North Shore near Point Venture is pictured from Lakeway's south shore in 2009. It captures a view of where Lohmann's Bridge was once located. The Point Venture Condominiums are a dominant landmark of the North Shore. (Courtesy of North Shore Heritage and Cultural Society.)

In 2000, the Lago Vista Property Owners Association built the K-Oaks Clubhouse. The excellent facility is used continuously for community activities. (Courtesy of North Shore Heritage and Cultural Society.)

Local groups participated in planning the landscaping of the K-Oaks grounds. A deer sculpture by Dan Pogue sets off the entrance garden. An inviting butterfly garden provides charm to the back garden area. The Garden Club, contributors to the butterfly garden, organized in 1975. (Courtesy of North Shore Heritage and Cultural Society.)

The Seton North Shore/Lago Vista Outreach Associates was established in 1984. It is an educational, fund-raising, and public relations association that supports Seton Healthcare Network and focuses on the North Shore area. Through the years, funds raised from their annual gala and other events have filled such needs as equipment for the new Seton Medical Williamson, where members are shown at the dedication of the Lago Vista Room in the women's center. (Courtesy of Genny Kercheville.)

Marge Richards is the only living daughter of a Civil War veteran in Texas. She is pictured here in one of the historic dresses she wears to conventions and historic functions. She was born prematurely to a young mother who was the bride of an elderly man. After her retirement, Marge began working with the Carewear National Organization to sew and knit clothing for premature infants in hospitals. While residing at The Island on Lake Travis in Lago Vista, she furthered her interest in donating items for premature infants by forming a sewing group with like-minded individuals. Marge remains very active, teaching adult Sunday school classes, swimming, playing bridge, and organizing events. In 2009, Marge was 95 years old. (Courtesy of North Shore Heritage and Cultural Society.)

The North Shore community loves to travel in groups. Lago Vista members attended the Sertoma Club District Meeting in Louisiana. A trip to Mardi Gras added adventure. For many years, Sally Lorenz organized bus trips (above) to Laredo, Mexico, for shopping and fun. More recent community excursions have explored cruises coordinated by Betty Jones through Austin Travel with Vicki Wood. (Courtesy of Shirley Davis.)

Bridge, bridge, and more bridge is being played daily on the North Shore. The Thursday Women's Duplicate Bridge Group, which meets at the Lago Vista Activity Center, has been playing together every week for 25 years. (Courtesy of Shirley Davis.)

Numerous civic and social groups offer challenging and interesting opportunities. Keep Lago Vista Beautiful, Lago Vista Women's Club, Lady Lakers Sandy Kahn and Leslie Winn (above) and Lago Vista Garden Club (below) are community organizations that believe in having fun as they enrich the community. (Both, courtesy of Shirley Davis.)

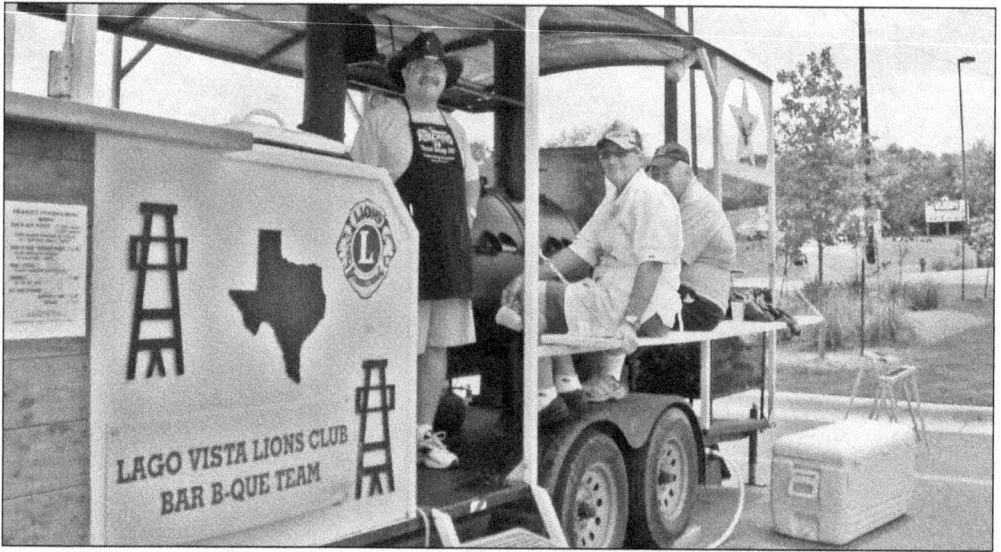

Lago Vista Lions Club (above) and Point Venture's Lions Clubs remain dedicated service-oriented groups who believe in having fun. One fund-raiser in 2009 was hosting Saturday barbecues at the Super S parking lot. All profits are donated to worthy causes. (Courtesy of North Shore Heritage and Cultural Society.)

Music group Firehouse Five, Plus or Minus (Firehouse 5+/–), was one of the early local musical groups to perform in the newly developing community. The group originally played benefits for the volunteer fire department's fund-raisers and other groups in the Lago Vista area. Later the band played for many dances and private parties. The group remains proud of the recognition it received. Mayor Rusty Allen declared by proclamation a Firehouse 5+/– Day on July 4, 1996. The band received the Unsung Hero award and later a certificate of appreciation from the Lions Club. Gene Markley published an article in the book Lago Vista: Its Story and Its People that gives a wonderful background of the band and its members. (Courtesy of the Markley family.)

Football at Sizemore Field has become a Friday night event. Within a few short years, athletic director and head football coach Alan Haire has taken an infant program to 2009 district champions. Jerry Sizemore, a National Football League Hall of Fame player, not only shares his name with the Lago Vista Football Program but has worked to make the school district a success by serving as a member on the school board. Despite adversity, Lago clinched the District 25-2A title. (Courtesy of *North Lake Travis LOG*.)

Lago Vista Women's Club (LVWC) is a vital organization on the North Shore of Lake Travis. The LVWC 2009 Lago Vista High School scholarship winners proudly wave to community members during the July Fourth Parade and Celebration. In addition to their scholarship awards, Rachel Duran (left) was salutatorian and Britney Mosely (right) was homecoming queen. (Courtesy of Vasara Photography.)

2009 UIL AA CX DEBATE STATE CHAMPIONS
MEGAN MUMFORD   COACH ERIC HOLT   DUNCAN HALL
WWW.VASARAPHOTOGRAPHY.COM

The evidence of academic success is the gold medals worn by the Lago Vista High School debate team after they won the 2009 state championship. (Courtesy of Vasara Photography.)

The Highland Lakes Golf Course and Club House functioned as many things. The elegant structure housed events ranging from casual golf celebrations to elegant country club functions. The swimming pool became the place for swimming lessons. While awaiting completion of the Lago Vista High School, students started the 1974–1975 school year in the clubhouse. (Courtesy of North Shore Heritage and Cultural Society.)

Marble Falls High School student musician Russell Garrett performed at the White House in December 2008 at the invitation of Pres. George W. Bush. Russell, son of Jim and Debbie Garrett, is a fourth-generation Travis Peak resident and a member of the Marble Falls High School choir. He is shown here holding a photograph of the choir from their performance. Russell is also a 2009 recipient of a scholarship to Abilene Christian University in drama and voice. (Courtesy of Jim and Debbie Garrett and Janice McGrew.)

C. C. Mason, the namesake of Leander Independent School District's fifth elementary school, was the founder of the Bagdad community. According to local historian Karen Thompson, Mason was the largest landowner of the area and surveyed most of the surrounding countryside. Mason was also instrumental in starting the Bagdad school, which subsequently became the Leander School and then the Leander Independent School District. Perhaps his most important legacy was hiring the first schoolteacher of the local public school district. The campus was dedicated on September 6, 1994. C. C. Mason faculty and staff enjoy a close relationship with the surrounding community, which includes students from the Jonestown area. (Courtesy of North Shore Heritage and Cultural Society.)

Lindsay Carmichael, a Lago Vista High School graduate, won a bronze medal in Women's Archery Competition in 2008 Paralympics hosted in Beijing, China. (Courtesy of *North Lake Travis LOG*.)

The Lago Vista City Sports Complex, built in 2003 on Bar-K Drive, features an Olympic-size swimming pool as part of its facilities. Lago Vista Independent School District and community members use the pool, sports fields, and tennis courts. A heritage kiosk houses panels that tell the history of the North Shore. (Courtesy of Nathan Scott Photography.)

The Primavera Bike Race is a sports competition held in Lago Vista. The spring race features a challenging course that loops around the Highland Lakes Estates terrain. The curvy hill country quest is a two-day event with competitors grouped into three categories: age, gender, and ability. Hollace Bowden, a volunteer and community leader known as "Mr. Lago Vista," was instrumental in starting and managing the race from its 1980s inception as the Tour of Texas bicycle race with international competitors to its 2008 form as the Primavera Bike Race. Hiram Everetts, a Lago Vista resident and Wisconsin state bicycling champion from 1923 to 1926, was a medal presenter in past years. From left to right above are Lago Vista police officer Luis Valdez, Hollace Bowden, Don Hutchinson, cyclist Matt Ankney, Lago Vista police officer Lawrence Jonap, and Lago Vista mayor Randy Kruger. (Courtesy of *North Lake Travis LOG*.)

Boating on Lake Travis takes place all year, but Memorial Day marks the start of the true summer season. The Austin Yacht Club's Sailboat Regatta entries finish their race at Bar-K. Devil's Hollow (below), with its deep cove, attracts boats of all types and sizes, and many remain anchored in the cove for days, weekends, and even longer. A festive spirit prevails, with music, parties, swimming, fishing, and other active and relaxing activities. Boats anchored in the cove have a prime view of evening fireworks provided by establishments located across the lake, such as Carlos and Charlie's. (Left, courtesy of the Markley family; below, courtesy of the Kelton Jones family.)

The joy of sailing is evident in this view of a fully engaged spinnaker. Both large and small boats enjoy sailing on Lake Travis. The skilled yachtsmen calculate each move as sailing craft are tested by the vagaries of the wind. (Courtesy of the Markley family.)

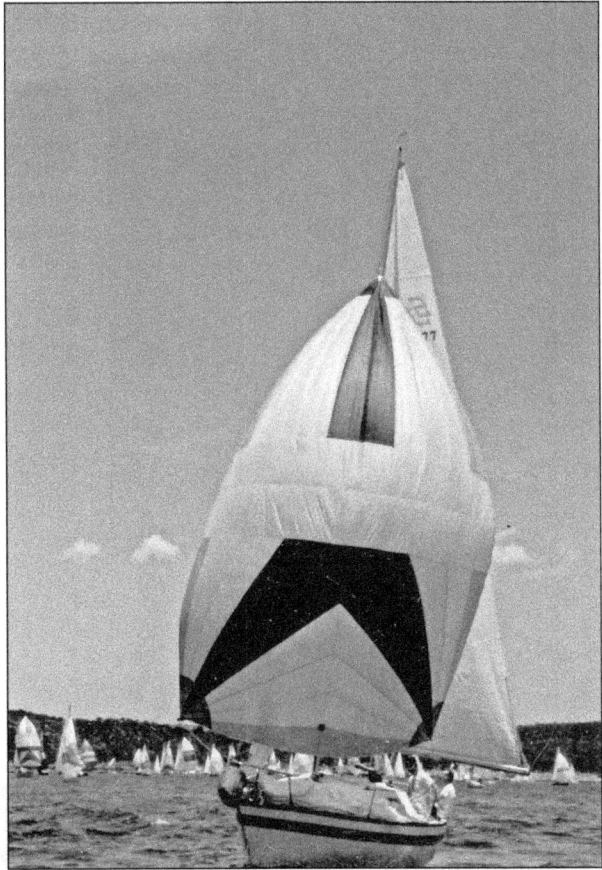

Amanda Casey (second from front) enjoys a weekend of sailing on her family's boat. Six senior classmates from Baylor University join her in 2009. (Courtesy of Sun Hi Casey.)

Hill Country Singers, long known for their outstanding performances in Lago Vista, perform in 2008 under the direction of Bill Parcher at the Texas State Capitol as elementary school students watch. Parcher works to expand the performing arts with his Twilight concert series performed at the Villa Antonia. (Courtesy of *North Lake Travis LOG*.)

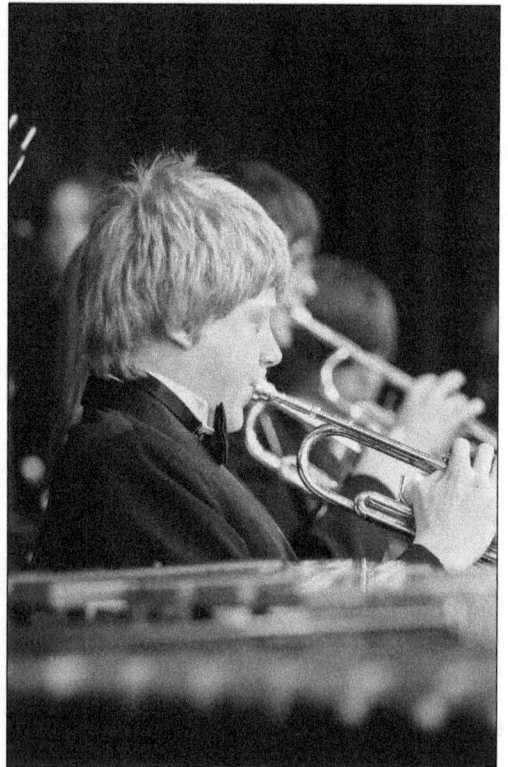

The hallmark of the 2008 Christmas season was a spirited performance at the Bar-K Clubhouse by Lago Vista High School musicians. Taylor Weaver is shown decked out in formal attire as he performs. (Courtesy of Vasara Photography.)

Nine

DEVELOPMENT-VILLE

Reflections of the times are seen everywhere: in the hills, on the shorelines, and along the recently expanded four-lane highway, FM 1431. Mansions with lake views, like the homes built in the Hollows development, replace fishing camps. Numerous luxury homes and condominium developments are nestled on the once-sparse landscape and waterfront. As new businesses found a secure market, the one-bank area has grown to have five banks. (Courtesy of North Shore Heritage and Cultural Society.)

Daughter Donna Jo Carter Priem and mother Betty Jo Jones Carter hold a distinguished position in the history of Jonestown. Jones and Carter Realtors is located on FM 1431 in a home built over 100 years ago. (Courtesy of North Shore Heritage and Cultural Society.)

Oski's Shopping Center took on a modern look in 2008 with a new roof and exterior update. As one of the oldest and most successful businesses in Lago Vista, it has housed many other businesses under its shopping center roof. (Courtesy of Genny Kercheville.)

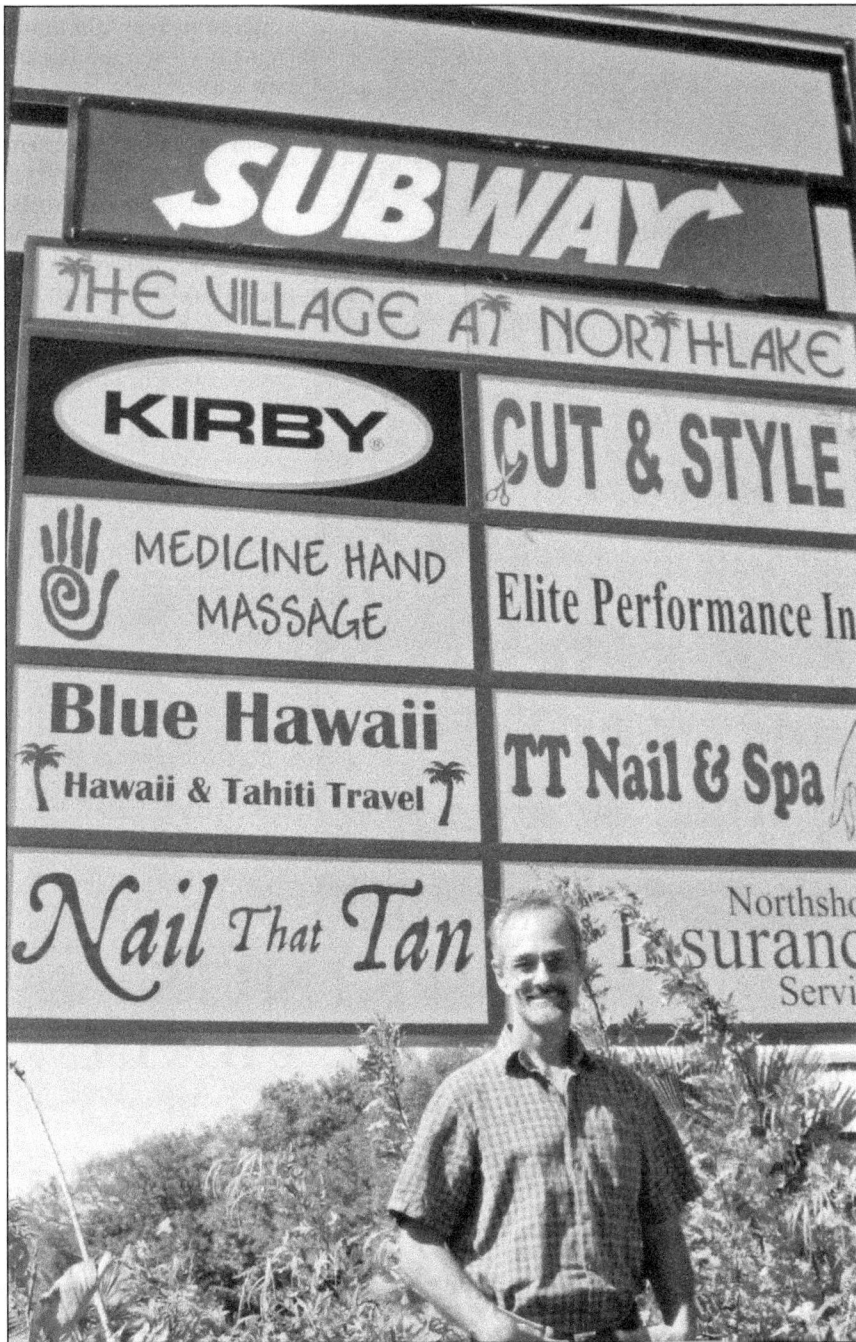

James Quinn is pictured here under the sign that displays the businesses located in the Village of Northlake in Jonestown. He first visited the area while on a high school trip. It took him 19 years to figure out a way to return to the beautiful hill country that he had fallen in love with on that high school trip. He bought the property that was originally called the Webb Café. During the late 1940s and early 1950s, it is rumored that they had a back room with cabinets whose doors opened to reveal slot machines. Jo Brower owned the property in the 1960s. Being a stone mason, he remodeled the building. (Courtesy of Janice McGrew.)

Interesting rock cliff formations remain a dominant feature along the edge of Lake Travis. Adding to this natural landscape, spacious homes have been built with elevators and paths leading to private marinas and boats. They can be seen nestled side by side in lakeside coves. (Courtesy of North Shore Heritage and Cultural Society.)

Change surrounded the North Shore of Lake Travis in 2009. School enrollment soared, home development projects multiplied, highways expanded, and new businesses were welcomed. All enriched the hill country landscape. Lago Vista High School's Viking volleyball team was part of the excitement. (Courtesy of Vasara Photography.)

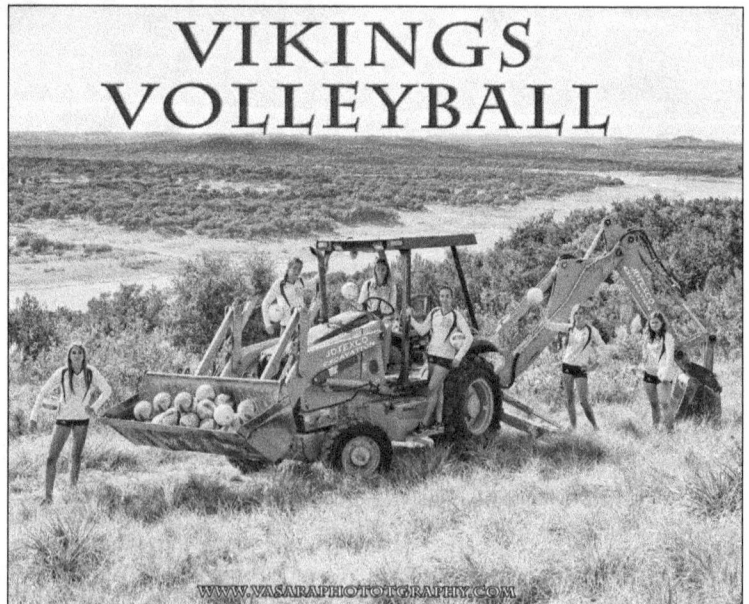

VIKINGS VOLLEYBALL

WWW.VASARAPHOTOTGRAPHY.COM

Interior roads and home development continue to carve into the landscape of the North Shore. (Courtesy of North Shore Heritage and Cultural Society.)

FM 1431 continues to be straightened and expanded to improve accessibility, which is highly valued by residents and visitors. What was once a dirt road with cattle gates now sports multiple lanes and modern landscaping. New roads and bridges are creating easier pathways to meet the needs of population growth and expansion on the North Shore. (Courtesy of North Shore Heritage and Cultural Society.)

The community's desire for more restaurants resulted in new eating places. Domino's and Tugs joined Sonic as favorite fast food locations by 2009. (Courtesy of North Shore Heritage and Cultural Society.)

With the opening of CVS Pharmacy in 2005, prescriptions could be obtained locally. Neighbors enjoyed meeting as they shopped in the new store. (Courtesy of North Shore Heritage and Cultural Society.)

Super S Supermarket opened in 2007. The event was celebrated with an appearance by Nolan Ryan, who was welcomed there to endorse his meat products. (Courtesy of *North Lake Travis LOG*.)

Super S Supermarket and the shopping mall quickly became a center of activities for shoppers. (Courtesy of North Shore Heritage and Cultural Society.)

Waterford Estates (above) makes an impressive hillside scene. The gated community boasts landscaped grounds, beautiful homes overlooking the lake, and friendly neighbors. One of the newest homes is shown below. (Both, courtesy of North Shore Heritage and Cultural Society.)

A newly built estate on Ivean Pearson Road displays many exceptional features. The main entrance is fashioned with European-styled ironwork and Italian marble columns that were handcrafted in China. Both the gate and fence are intricately embellished. On the property is a 9,000 square foot guest house with 10 bedrooms and 12 bathrooms. Other unique features include a bowling alley, movie theater, an enclosed boat marina, professional tennis courts, and a spa. (Courtesy of North Shore Heritage and Cultural Society.)

Flat Creek Estate winery and vineyards are located in the shadow of the well-known landmark, Travis Peak. Rick and Madelyn Naber purchased the premier 80 acres from Roy and Patsy Koontz in 1999 and began the development. Original farm equipment, buildings, and a pecan orchard remain as part of the estate. Flat Creek Estate has won international acclaim for its select wines. Four new Texas limestone buildings with a western flair provide space for numerous activities. Guests can enjoy wine tasting, eating, entertainment, meeting rooms, and an outdoor pavilion for concerts and cultural events. The beauty of the vineyards enhances the land while native grasses, wildflowers, birds, and wildlife continue to thrive. (Courtesy of *North Lake Travis LOG*.)

Drs. Shannon Kerns and Mark Dworsky cut the ribbon to mark the grand opening of North Shore Eyecare in 2009. (Courtesy of *North Lake Travis LOG*.)

120

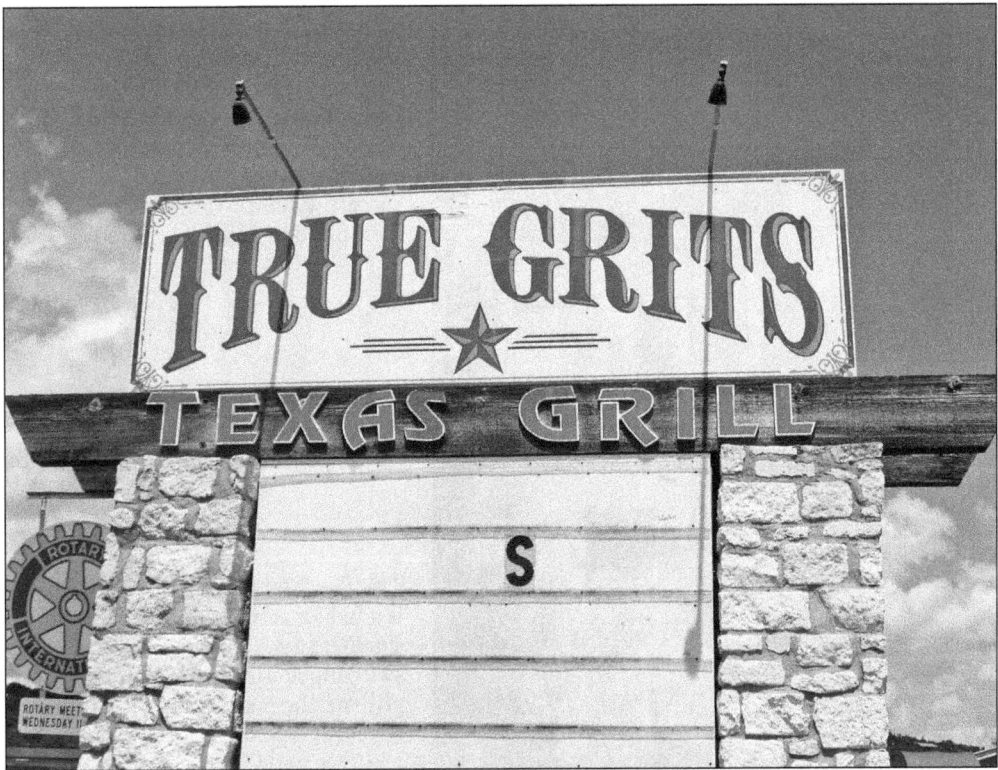

True Grits Restaurant, located in Jonestown on FM 1431, is popular for its good food and ranch atmosphere. (Courtesy of North Shore Heritage and Cultural Society.)

Dee Dee's Restaurant and Caterers serves authentic Mexican food in Lago Vista near the intersection of FM 1431 and Lohmann Road. (Courtesy of North Shore Heritage and Cultural Society.)

The mall that waited to be completed held everyone's curiosity, but numerous delays postponed its opening. Residents dealing with growth pains were eagerly waiting and hoping for success. (Courtesy of North Shore Heritage and Cultural Society.)

The Pier Restaurant in Point Venture is a hub of activity during the summer season. Boats, swimsuits, swinging music, and food from the grill are the perfect mix for a fun time. (Courtesy of North Shore Heritage and Cultural Society.)

The Casey Professional Building is a classic Texas Tuscan architectural success that complements Lago Vista with a solid, rich appearance. Doug and Sun Hi Casey have exquisitely planned both exterior and interior construction designs and included original artwork by Sun Hi. Pictured from left to right below are the Casey team, Marilyn Gietl, Brian Adams, and Sun Hi and Doug Casey, in the interior of the Casey Professional Building with a fusion glass mural. (Above, courtesy of the North Shore Heritage and Cultural Society; below, courtesy of Macy Hurwitz with the *North Lake Travis LOG*.)

There was much to celebrate when Luisa Velazquez Lopez (left) opened Luisa's Beauty Shop in 2007. A mariachi band played music, and delicious food was shared with family and friends. Luisa and her husband, Enrique Lopez (right), are pictured with their daughters, Marlen Lopez (front left) and Luisa Fernanda Lopez (front right), in front of the mariachi band. Enrique's business, Avalar Real Estate Office, is currently located beside Luisa's Beauty Shop. (Courtesy of Luisa Lopez.)

Salutatorian of the Lago Vista High School class of 1979, Kelly Van Cleave set her sights on performing and graduated from Southwest Texas State University with a degree in theater arts and a minor in education. Since that time, she has performed as a circus arena physical comedian in national and international venues. After auditioning and being selected for Ringling Brothers Barnum and Bailey Circus Clown College, she performed with that circus for four years. She later performed in the Americano Circus in Europe and Circus Circus in Las Vegas, Nevada. Presently she is performing with Kinoshita Circus in Japan, where her photograph appeared on the cover of *Heal the World Institute* magazine, published on the occasion of the 100th anniversary of the Kinoshita Circus. (Courtesy of the Van Cleave family.)

Many of the Rodgers family members live on the North Shore on parts of the Sunset Ranch, which will mark its centennial year of existence in 2011. The family of George H. "Buddy" and Margaret Rodgers is pictured together at the Sunset Ranch in 2009 at the home of Dick and Genny Kercheville. It was on this same site that George Lunsford established his homestead and built a log cabin with a limestone rock fireplace in 1890. Stone fences, old rustic farming equipment, and the tin barn remind residents of past occupants, and the shade of the big live oak trees provides comfort for yet another appreciative generation on this historic site. (Courtesy of Genny Kercheville.)

Lake Travis resort areas remain a popular place for anglers, boaters, campers, and swimmers. The Lower Colorado River Authority has parks and preserves in abundance. Parks include Shaffer Bend, Narrows, Grelle, Turkey Bend, and Muleshoe Bend. Preserves include McGregor, Westcave, and Wheless. Travis County parks near the North Shore of Lake Travis also offer adventure. They include Pace Bend, Arkansas Bend, and Sandy Creek. At left, Mike Sanders enjoys fishing during his Christmas break in 2008. The Lake Travis enclosed fishing well (below) is heated and air-conditioned, and catfish weighing over 20 pounds have been caught there. (Left, courtesy of the Sanders family; below, courtesy of National Resort Communities.)

The Balcones Canyonlands National Wildlife Refuge (BCNWR), located on the North Shore, preserves endangered treasures. Birders from around the world come to sight the treasured birds, native plants, primitive fossils, and habitats that are protected by the refuge. Dr. Chuck Sexton, refuge biologist, is a popular presenter during the yearly songbird festival held in the spring. Land protection programs of parks, preserves, and the BCNWR have further defined the North Shore as an environmental paradise. The tremendous benefits gained are appreciated by the local communities. Two endangered songbirds are protected by the BCNWR natural habitat—the golden-cheeked warbler and the black-capped vireo. (Courtesy of the Goch Family.)

Visit us at
arcadiapublishing.com